J. *Gaberell, Zürich*

WEGGIS IN THE SPRING

THE CRADLE OF SWITZERLAND

THE CRADLE OF SWITZERLAND

By

ARNOLD LUNN

LONDON

HOLLIS & CARTER

MADE AND PRINTED IN GREAT BRITAIN AT
THE CHAPEL RIVER PRESS, ANDOVER, HANTS, FOR
HOLLIS & CARTER LTD., 25 ASHLEY PLACE, LONDON, S.W.1

First published 1952
3.52

TO JIMMY PALMER-TOMKINSON

MY DEAR DORIS,

I had passed the proofs of this dedication page before your husband, Jimmy, was killed by a high-speed crash into rocks while practising for the British Ski Championship. The courage he always showed as a racer was matched by your amazing fortitude after the accident, which you witnessed.

My job as manager of the Team was a sinecure while Jimmy was captain. His influence on the younger racers, due in part to his great prestige as a racer, was invaluable in matters more important than ski-ing. He hated the word " sportsmanship," because it has been so degraded, and for this reason I prefer to use the word " chivalry " to suggest his greatest contribution to the Teams which he captained. He was incapable of an ungenerous thought or of an unchivalrous action. In the many difficult situations which are inevitable in international sport he had an unerring instinct for the right decision.

No British racer was more beloved in the ski-racing world, a little world which is sadly impoverished by his death. To have known him is " part of life's unalterable good."

You, who were born a Swiss, will sympathize with my motive in writing this book, to promote a better understanding of the cultural background of the enchanting country which Jimmy regarded as his second home.

ARNOLD LUNN
21 *January*, 1952

LIST OF ILLUSTRATIONS

WEGGIS IN THE SPRING	*frontispiece*
	facing page
BROTHER KLAUS' ALTAR AT SACHSELN	98
ENGELBERG IN WINTER	99
MELCHSEE-FRUTT. TITLIS IN THE BACK-GROUND	114
THE JESUIT CHURCH, LUCERNE	115
THE BÜRGENSTOCK	178
THE URI-ROTHSTOCK, FROM AXENSTEIN ABOVE BRUNNEN	179
ANDERMATT, LOOKING TOWARDS THE FURKA	210
EINSIEDELN, LOOKING DOWN THE NAVE	211

CONTENTS

PAGE

PREFACE xi

PART I

HISTORICAL BACKGROUND

CHAPTER

I INTRODUCING LAKE LUCERNE
1. The Tyranny of Fashion . . . 3
2. The Lake of the Forest Cantons . 5

II THE HOME OF THE HABSBURGS
1. The Holy Roman Empire . . 13
2. The Rise of the Habsburgs . . 17

III THE IMMORTAL MEADOW
1. The Rütli Legend 22
2. Europe in the Thirteenth Century . 23
3. The Importance of the St. Gotthard
Pass 28
4. The Strategy of the Forest Cantons . 29
5. William Tell—History or Legend? . 32
6. August 1st, 1291 34

IV THE DECISIVE BATTLES 37

V THE CENTRAL CANTONS AND THE REFOR-
MATION
1. Marignano and Zwingli . . . 43
2. The Religious Wars . . . 46
3. The Precarious Equilibrium . . 47
4. Foreign Alliances 48
5. Swiss Neutrality 50

vii

CHAPTER   PAGE

VI   NAPOLEONIC INTERLUDE
     1. Switzerland in the Eighteenth Century   52
     2. Impatient Liberators   .   .   53
     3. Stratford Canning in Switzerland   .   57

VII   A VERY CIVIL WAR   63

VIII   WHY DEMOCRACY WORKS IN SWITZERLAND
     1. Imperilled Democracy   .   .   .   67
     2. The Swiss Constitution   .   .   .   68
     3. The Modest Rôle of Swiss Politicians .   72
     4. *Kantönligeist*   75
     5. Swiss Prosperity   .   .   .   77

IX   THE LIFE OF AN ALPINE VALLEY
     1. The Alps   80
     2. Village Oligarchies .   .   .   82

PART II

THE CONTEMPORARY SCENE

X   BRUDER KLAUS' COUNTRY
     1. The Brünig Pass   .   .   .   87
     2. Bruder Klaus   .   .   .   89
     3. The church at Sachseln   .   .   95
     4. Sarnen   98

XI   STANS AND ENGELBERG
     1. Stans and Stansstad   .   .   100
     2. Engelberg   101
     3. An Eighteenth-Century Whig visits
        Engelberg   103
     4. Engelberg and the English   .   .   105

XII   MELCHSEE-FRUTT
     1. The Lake   107
     2. A Memorable Day .   .   .   109
     3. Other Melchsee Memories   .   .   111
     4. *O Lobä, Zuä Lobä*   .   .   .   114

CHAPTER   PAGE

XIII   THE TOWN OF LUCERNE
       1. Introductory   115
       2. The Hofkirche   117
       3. Lucerne North of the Reuss   .   .   118
       4. Lucerne South of the Reuss   .   .   120
       5. The Famous Bridges   .   .   .   124
       6. Wagner and the Villa Tribschen   .   126
       7. The Bourbaki Panorama   .   .   .   129
       8. The Glacier Garden   .   .   .   132

XIV   THE LION OF LUCERNE
       1. The " Zapolotes "   .   .   .   133
       2. The Swiss Regiments in France   .   136
       3. The Swiss Regiments in the Service of
              Holland and Great Britain   .   .   141
       4. The Men Commemorated by the Lion
              of Lucerne   143
       5. The Controversy Provoked by the
              Lion of Lucerne   .   .   .   147
       6. Advantages and Disadvantages   .   148
       7. The Swiss Guard   .   .   .   152

XV   PILATUS AND BÜRGENSTOCK
       1. Pilatus   155
       2. The Bürgenstock   .   .   .   157

XVI   THE RIGI AND THE RIGI RIVIERA   .   .   162
       1. Weggis, Vitznau and Gersau   .   .   162
       2. The Rigi   165

XVII BRUNNEN   169
       1. Schiller's William Tell   .   .   169
       2. Shelley at Brunnen .   .   .   173
       3. Days at Brunnen   .   .   .   176
       4. Expeditions from Brunnen   .   .   178

XVIII " THE UNBOUGHT GRACE OF LIFE "
       1. The Ital Reding House .   .   .   181
       2. Schwyz, Town and Canton   .   .   185

CHAPTER	PAGE
XIX ZUG	
1. Early History	187
2. Old Buildings in Zug	188
3. Churches in Zug	189
4. Goethe at Zug	190
XX THE ST. GOTTHARD FROM FLÜELEN TO GÖSCHENEN	
1. Brunnen to Flüelen	192
2. Altdorf	194
3. Amsteg and Göschenen	194
XXI "STOCKINGS WITH SHORTS"	196
XXII ANDERMATT AND THE ST. GOTTHARD PASS	202
1. The History of the St. Gotthard Pass	203
2. Suvoroff and the St. Gotthard	206
3. Historic Highways	208
4. The Recurring Pattern	208
XXIII EINSIEDELN	211
1. St. Meinrad	211
2. The Charm of Baroque	213
3. The Interior of the Abbey	214
APPENDIX: MOTORING DISTANCES IN MILES	
1. The Approaches to Central Switzerland	222
2. The Motoring Passes of Central Switzerland	222
3. The Lake of Lucerne and Neighbourhood	223
INDEX	224

PREFACE

1890

NEARLY sixty years have passed since I first spent a summer on the shores of Lake Lucerne. I know the five Cantons described in this book as a mountaineer and as a skier. I have walked and skied, motored and bicycled across their passes. I fell in love with the incomparable beauty of the mountains and lakes of Central Switzerland in my youth, and as the years passed I began to discover the treasures of art and architecture in the five Cantons.

Many books about Switzerland have been written by men for whom Switzerland is nothing more than an arena for athletic achievement, and the counterpart of those who are uninterested in Switzerland below the snow line are the historians who are equally uninterested in Switzerland above the snow line. Sport has to be disinfected by age before it is accepted as a suitable subject for academic treatment, and serious historians would lose caste if they mentioned any athletic events later than the classic Olympic Games, but the resolute refusal of every Swiss historian whom I have read to mention mountaineering or ski-ing is perhaps an instinctive reaction against the over-emphasis on Switzerland as " The Playground of Europe," to quote the infelicitous title of Leslie Stephen's delightful book. I have every sympathy with the Swiss who resent the widespread belief that their remarkable little country is mainly interesting as a kind of International Fun Fair, but it is unhistorical to ignore the decisive importance of the discovery of mountain beauty in the eighteenth, of mountain adventure in the nineteenth, and of winter sports in the twentieth century.

The tourist business represents one of the most important of Swiss invisible exports, and no historian of the Swiss can afford to ignore the social revolution, partly beneficial and partly mischievous, which the tourist invasion provoked in remote Alpine valleys. And surely the interpretation of mountain romance in literature and in art, as for instance in the poetry of Byron and Wordsworth, in the prose of Ruskin and Leslie Stephen, and in the art of Turner, Calame and Segantini, is of greater significance than the development of the watch industry or the evolution of Pestalozzi's ideas about education.

Though I am interested in Switzerland both above and below the snow line, in this book I am mainly concerned to provide a corrective to the " playground of Europe " conception of Switzerland. This book will, I hope, be of use to the kind of traveller who is interested in the historical background, literary associations and artistic treasures of the countries which he visits, but who lacks the necessary leisure for prolonged research before starting out on his travels. The book is accordingly divided into two parts. Part I is an outline history of the Five Cantons which gives, I hope, the essential facts. As almost all the decisive events in the history of Switzerland have either taken place within, or had important repercussions on, the Five Cantons, these earlier chapters might be mistaken for a digest of Swiss history, but the result is accidental and not intended. It is difficult to make a digest of history very readable, and I suggest that the reader who is contemplating his first visit to the Cradle of Switzerland, might begin at Part II, Chapter X, and read the regional chapters first.

The Swiss concentrate on advertising their incomparable scenery and are therefore partially responsible for the illusion that Switzerland is a mere country of transit for travellers in search of the artistic treasures of Italy. It would be idle to pretend that Switzerland is as rich in art and architecture as Italy or France, but it is not only the Abbey of Einsiedeln, considered by good judges to be the best baroque church north of the Alps, which attracts the connoisseurs of Baroque and Renaissance architecture to the Five Cantons. I commend to specialists the cantonal monographs on art and architecture, and in particular Dr. L. Birchler's monumental work on Schwyz.

In conclusion I should like to record my indebtedness to Herr Martin Mengelt, who encouraged me to write this book; to Dr. R. E. Schazmann, the director of the Bibliothèque Nationale Suisse, not only for obtaining permission for me to borrow books but also for drawing my attention to many rare historical pamphlets. I am also very grateful to my wife and to my friends Douglas Woodruff and Phyllis Holt-Needham who read the manuscript and gave me many valuable suggestions.

ARNOLD LUNN

PART I

HISTORICAL BACKGROUND

Chapter I

INTRODUCING LAKE LUCERNE

1. The Tyranny of Fashion

THE tyranny of fashion is as irresistible in culture as in women's clothes, and it is difficult to remember that the Lake of Lucerne once had an esoteric appeal comparable to that which Argos or Ravenna possesses to-day. Goethe, who has some claim to be regarded as the founder of Neo-Hellenism, never visited Greece, but he made three journeys to the Lake of Lucerne, and it was Goethe who suggested to Schiller that William Tell would be a splendid subject for an epic. To the eighteenth-century intellectuals Morgarten was as romantic as Marathon. If Gibbon had been a better German scholar he would have completed the story of Switzerland's birth which he began, instead of writing the story of Rome's decline. " There is one theme," he wrote in 1762, " which I should prefer to all others, *the history of the liberty of the Swiss*, of that independence which a brave people rescued from the House of Austria, defended against the Dauphin of France, and finally sealed with the blood of Charles of Burgundy."

When Shelley ran away from his wife he chose for his illicit honeymoon Brunnen which, to the modern poet, is a station where the Gotthard Express makes a brief halt on its way to Italy. Now the mountains are as lovely as they ever were, and the historical associations which attracted Shelley to Lucerne have been uneroded by time. And if you regard luxury hotels as a blot on the landscape, there are many quiet lakeside or mountain resorts where the hotels are no larger than in Shelley's day. " Has this hotel changed much," I asked a hotelier at Brienz, " since Byron stopped here? " " Oh yes," she replied, rather nettled by the implied reflection, " we've put running water in every room." " But in Shelley's day," you may object, " there were no cheap trippers." " Mont Blanc at sunset," wrote Oscar Wilde, " flushes like a rose, with shame, perhaps at the prevalence of tourists." There are of course tourists, Oscar Wilde for instance, who might well provoke an alpine blush, and it is amusing to note that people who talk like this always regard themselves as an exception to their pet generalisation that Switzerland has been ruined by the influx of foreigners.

The modern attitude of the intelligentsia to Switzerland cannot be explained by the influx of tourists, for tourists have also invaded Italy, and it is as easy to escape from tourists in little Swiss towns such as Sempach or Romont as in little Italian towns such as Lucca or Arezzo. There are hill cities in Switzerland whose embattled towers remind one of a Dürer etching, cities whose ancient peace is untroubled by tourist charabancs, towns where

The wind is astir in the arches with the sound of swords unseen
And the cry is of kings departed, and of battles that have been.

Nobody who " remembers Europe and the centuries " can have much patience with the repetitive clichés of those whose attitude to Switzerland is determined not by history but by fashion. From the summit of the Rigi you will no doubt see the approach of a train-load of tourists winding its way up the mountain side, but you will also see the lakes which witnessed the first tentative beginnings of civilisation, and the undulating plains across which ran the great military roads of Rome, roads along which the Caesars posted on their journeys from the Tiber to the distant Rhine. Those plains re-echoed to the tramp of the Roman and the Goth, the Hun, the Austrian and the Burgundian. Few great military geniuses have set their mark on Europe without crossing this Alpine land. Emperors and bishops, pilgrims and merchants, have toiled across the Alpine passes from the Germanies to the gentler South. Within the frontiers of Switzerland, quarrels were debated and decided which changed the map of Europe. Had not Burgundy been defeated near the waters of Neuchâtel there might to-day be a Central European kingdom between Germany and France; but the dream of that buffer state went down before the halberds of the Swiss. From the Habisburg, a little castle in Northern Switzerland, there rode forth a man who claimed the Imperial Crown, and whose descendants ruled at one time over Spain and the Netherlands, Germany and Austria. In the foothills near Lucerne that same royal family was defeated by the sturdy peasants of the Forest Cantons, the first great defeat of feudalism.

"For centuries since Roman times," wrote Frederic Harrison, "few who leave their own country fail to find themselves there (in Switzerland). And, for at least two, if not three centuries European literature and poetry ring with its local memories."

2. The Lake of the Forest Cantons

It was not until I had seen the mountains and lakes of the Rockies and the Andes that I fully realised how much the Alpine lakes owe to their historical associations. Lucerne would be world-famous even if Switzerland had produced nothing but cuckoo clocks, for its natural beauties are unrivalled. I wish I could find words to describe its peculiar charm.

It is not a mere literary conceit to find analogies between scenery and architecture. In my book *Switzerland and the English* I have tried to trace the relationship between classical architecture and the kind of scenery which classical men enjoyed.   Ruskin's memorable phrase " the look of mountain brotherhood between the Cathedral and the Alp " helps us to understand why the dawn of the mountain cult in the eighteenth century coincided with the Gothic revival, for rugged mountains are examples of what may be called " Gothic landscape."   It is no accident that the same prophet—Ruskin—should have created a fashion both for the Gothic Aiguilles of Chamonix and also for Gothic architecture.

From the terraces of San Remigio above Pallanza, you look out on to a majestic sweep of unimpeded water towards the ordered sequence of the hills that lean towards Lombardy.   " There is room in that air and space for dreams."   Maggiore is classical landscape but Lake Lucerne is pure Gothic.   The mountains which rise from its waters do not suggest the precise and careful finish of the classical architecture but the vigour of execution and fertility of invention of the Gothic architects and Gothic craftsmen.

It is perhaps significant that Lake Garda which is as " classical " as Maggiore should have inspired the first classical poem in praise of a mountain lake—Catullus's lovely lyric in which he celebrated his return to the laughter of Garda's wavelets, but not one of the many thousands of Romans who saw the Gothic lakes of central Switzerland has left on record one line of tribute to their beauty.

Your first introduction to the lake should be made by boat.   There are few things more enjoyable than to spend a day travelling from Lucerne to Flüelen and back to Lucerne.   The rhythmic splash as the propeller churns the lake water has a mesmeric quality.   The sound blends imperceptibly with the slow rhythm of the mountains that gradually disclose themselves.   As the steamer rounds the promontory of Meggen, which divides the bays of Lucerne and Küssnacht, you can see on the north shore a statue of

Christ with outstretched arms, half hidden by the trees, the gift of a mother whose daughter was drowned near this spot. I never noticed this statue until my wife pointed it out. The Christ seems as if He had come down a path through the trees and paused at the edge of the lake, with arms outstretched in welcome. Often when the tracer bullets and searchlights were weaving their macabre pattern on the skies of war-tormented London our thoughts returned to the Christ of Meggen, and to the tranquil lake whose night waters mirrored the patient stars and not the flicker of bombers caught in the searchlight rays.

When the war had faded out into the cold war I spent an April morning beside the waters of Galilee. The little red flowers, perhaps the " lilies " of the New Testament, were in full bloom and the creamy white of Hermon's snows recalled the tone and texture of the Rigi snows in spring. And I remembered the Christ of Meggen and saw quite plain that there was a necessary connection between the loveliness of mountain lakes in spring and the new thing which came into the world when the Romans were building their roads across this mountain land, that new thing of which St. Augustine wrote when, after conceding his immense indebtedness to the great writers of classical antiquity, he added, " But nobody heard in those books the voice of one saying, ' Come unto me all ye that travail and are heavy laden and I will refresh you '."

Between Lucerne and Brunnen the lake is in the form of a rough irregular cross, the two arms of which, the Alpnach and Küssnacht bays, disclose themselves just as the steamer passes the promontory of Meggen. The mountains which will close in on us again at Weggis open up, and something is added to the grandeur of the lake, a note of repose and of distance, as the eyes travel beyond the tender recession of the Brünig valley to the gleam of the triple-crested Wetterhorn, a pattern of white pyramids imposed on the blue distance of unending space.

The Rigi dominates the bay of Weggis and Vitznau, and of the Rigi the most striking feature is the great wall of reddish pudding-stone above the shelving green of grass terraces. The lake contracts at the " Nase " where a spur of the Bürgenstock all but meets a spur of the Rigi. The steamer crosses the lake to Buochs (whence you can reach Engelberg by tram) and then returns to the north shore at Gersau. At Brunnen the lake turns sharply south into the Urner See where tremendous cliffs are reflected and reversed in the narrow fiord-like waters of Uri. Sir James Mackintosh, who sailed up the lake in 1814, maintained that it was upon this part of the lake, the bay of Uri, that " its superiority to all other lakes or, as far as I know, scenes upon earth, depends. The vast mountains rising on every side and closing at the end, with their rich clothing of woods, the sweet soft shoots of verdant pasture scattered at their feet and sometimes on their breast, and the expanse of water unbroken by islands, and almost undisturbed by any signs of living men, make an impression which it would be foolish to attempt to convey by words."

Nobody can claim to know this enchanted lake until he has seen it in all the changing seasons. Ruskin, who spent Christmas at Lucerne in 1861, declared that " the finest things one can see in summer are nothing compared to winter scenery among the Alps when the weather is fine. Pilate looked as if it was entirely constructed of frosted silver, like Geneva filigree work—lighted by golden sunshine with long purple shadows, and the entire chain of the Alps rosy beyond."

At the beginning of March vivid splashes of young green on the southern slopes near the water's edge proclaim the resurrection of colour. As I write I remember an April week at Alpnach. The Wetterhorn showed between a tracery of cherry blossom, and there were gentians just above the lake, and a waterfall which in winter is a senile trickle, stumbling with uncertain step down pendent icicles, had been transformed by the renascent sun into a foam of triumphant water.

Summer is high season in the Alps, mainly, I suppose, because of the school holidays, but the Alps are lovelier in October than in August. The weather is usually more settled. The mellow, golden light of October subdues all distances and tones down the harsher contrasts, and is yet so crystal-clear that the details of distant ranges are revealed with a precision which, in summer, would augur the imminence of rain. It is this contrast of tenderness and clarity which is the chief glory of those long, unbroken weeks of sunshine which we associate with the Alpine autumn.

In October the mountain lakes are a miracle of subtle tone and texture. Pools of transparent green break up the surface of darker turquoise. The flat uniformity of the August lakes has given way to a mirror of changing lights and colour. From the water's edge rise the shoulders of the ancient hills, mantled in trees, purple and blood-red near the lakeside, and above, evergreens shot with the gold of the larch. In summer the larch merges into the pine, its individuality is lost against a background unredeemed in its monotony of green. But in October the pines are flecked with flaming larch; the larch has come into its own, and its burnished gold mocks the sober puritanism of the pine.

There is a charming passage in one of Matthew Arnold's letters in which he describes Lucerne in autumn. He writes:—

We have been at Lucerne, as the schools here are only just reopened, and I wanted to see something of those in a Catholic Canton. At Lucerne we had good weather, the first time I have ever had good weather at Lucerne, and certainly there is no more beautiful place in the whole world. And the blaze of colour now that the rain had brought the purple that was wanted, the bright green still of the pastures, the black green of the firs, the yellow gold of the poplars, walnuts, chestnuts, and wych elms, and the red gold of the beeches, and at the foot of it all the lake, and at the head of it all the snowy line with Titlis, a mountain for whom Obermann has always given me a peculiar interest: then Lucerne itself with its curtain of old wall and trees and bridges, and the broad blue-green Reuss going through it. It required a day of mist and rain and penetrating damp, showing what the late autumn and winter at Lucerne are, to make it possible for one to depart. Tommy and I took the steamer on Sunday afternoon to Alpnach: the Alpnach arm of the lake goes among the recesses of the mountains as the Küssnacht arm goes among the opener pastoral country; and I have never seen anything more impressive than Pilatus as we gradually half-rounded him, and more solemn than the whole folding in of the hills, at this autumnal season.

The influence of man on natural scenery is more often mischievous than beneficent, but on balance the Alps gain from the patina of human associations. The contrast, for instance, between Lake Lucerne and the Emerald Lake in Chile which is often compared with Lake Lucerne. The Lago Todos los Santos, to give the Emerald Lake its correct name, has, like Lucerne, a cruciform ground plan, narrow inlets and winding bays with sudden vistas of snow peaks and wooded hills, but the contrast between the two lakes is even more striking than their resemblances. It was not until I visited the Emerald Lake that I fully realised the importance of man as a geological agent.

Man has been at work for thousands of years round the shores of Lake Lucerne. He has carved the cattle alps out of the primeval forests, and thus provided not only the cow with pasture, but also the skier with open running. But man is a late-comer to the Chilean lakeland, and the slopes which rise from the Emerald Lake are choked and strangled with trees. Only a few scanty plots of green have been liberated from the dictatorship of the forests. And as the Fuji-esque volcano of glacier capped Orsono showed between the framework of coije trees I sighed for little villages nestling near the lake, for Gothic spires and weather-stained chalets, and friendly little paths leading through the forests to the smooth beauty of the cattle alps, and I realised as never before how much of the Alpine magic is due to cultural and historical associations, and I remembered Dr. Arnold's comment on the glorious view from St. Cergues, " One that I never saw surpassed, nor can I ever; for if America should afford scenes of greater natural beauty, yet the associations cannot be the same. No time, to civilised man, can make the Andes like the Alps; another Deluge alone could place them on a level."

The only criticism to be made of the best book ever written about mountaineering is that the title of Leslie Stephen's classic, *The Playground of Europe*, is grossly misleading. " Switzerland," wrote Frederic Harrison, " might be made one of the most instructive schools of history, one of the most exquisite schools of every sense of beauty, one of the most pathetic schools of spiritual wonder—and they make it a mere playground."

No lake, with the one supreme exception of Galilee, has nobler memories than the Lake of Lucerne or more varied literary associations. The Lake of Geneva is its only rival, and Geneva never witnessed, as did Lucerne, the birth of a nation. Modern Switzerland has been created and shaped by struggles whose issue was determined within, or on, the frontiers of the five Cantons which are the theme of this book. It was in the battles waged within a few miles of the lake that Switzerland was born. It was on the shores of this lake that the armies of revolutionary France met their most desperate opposition. It was these Cantons which won the decisive religious civil wars of the sixteenth and seventeenth centuries, and lost the Civil

War of 1847, the matrix from which modern Switzerland was born.

I had intended to introduce the appropriate historical background in the course of the book, describing, for instance, the beginnings of the Confederation in the chapter on Brunnen, the French invasion in the chapter on Unterwalden but, as I have pointed out in the Preface, everything of supreme importance for the development of Switzerland has either originated in or, as in the case of the Reformation, been bitterly opposed by these five Cantons, and it therefore seemed to me best to begin the book with a brief outline of Swiss history. Many of my mountaineering and ski-ing friends have suggested that I should write a brief history of Switzerland and I hope that the historical part of this book and the description of Swiss institutions will be read by skiers who have no immediate intention of visiting the five Cantons, and that it will serve to whet their appetite for the more solid fare provided by the great Swiss historians whom I have quoted in this book.

The English visitor is perplexed, and perhaps even faintly irritated, by the prosperity of this little country and uneasily aware that Swiss neutrality in two world wars is not the sole reason for the well-stocked shops and high standard of living. Some of the reasons for Swiss prosperity are suggested in Chapter VIII of this book.

May I conclude by expressing the hope that those who bought or borrowed this book because they are intending to visit the lovely places described in the later chapters will, at least, skim through Chapters II to VIII. Some knowledge of the historical and cultural background of the Five Cantons will add enormously to the pleasure of their holiday.

Chapter II

THE HOME OF THE HABSBURGS

1. The Holy Roman Empire

IF the hanging bridge which shortened the route over the St. Gotthard Pass had not been built, and if the St. Gotthard had not in consequence displaced the Lukmanier as the shortest route into Italy, and if the Habsburgs had retained the Imperial throne, Switzerland as an independent country would never have come into existence. The Swiss are Swiss and not Germans, French or Italians because the men of Uri controlled the St. Gotthard, and because the Emperor could not afford to allow the Habsburgs to control the key route into Italy. He therefore supported Uri, Schwyz and Unterwalden in their struggle against the Habsburgs.

It is impossible to understand the origins of Switzerland in general, and of the cradle of Switzerland in particular, without some understanding of the nature of the Holy Roman Empire, and some knowledge of the early history of the House of Habsburg. The roots of the Holy Roman Empire are to be found in the old Roman Empire. When the new Rome rose beside the banks of the Bosphorus, Constantinople became the centre of what has often inaccurately been termed the Empire of the East (A.D. 324). But in reality the Roman Empire was, and always continued to be, ideally one and indivisible. There were two Emperors but one Empire; two persons but one power. This point is of great importance for the understanding of the whole of the Middle Ages.

When the Church captured the Roman world the Empire was something more than a Government. It was a "fashion of conceiving the world." The doctrine that there is one Church of which Christ is the Head and we are all members, reinforced for Christians the conception of a necessary political unity of all the world under a single head. *Una chiesa in uno stato.*

The barbarians in the fifth century who all but broke up the Empire at least left the Universal Catholic Church intact, and with the Church the conception of the Empire.

Meanwhile, the divergence between East and West was becoming more pronounced. The Bishop of Rome was becoming more powerful, and his growing prestige rendered his position in subjection to the Emperor at Constantinople more and more incongruous. But the Popes still needed protection, not only from the Lombards, but also from the wild nobility of Rome. So they turned in this crisis in their fortunes to Charlemagne, King of the Franks, and summoned him to their assistance. In A.D. 800 Charlemagne was crowned Emperor of the West—not yet, be it noted, Holy Roman Emperor.

In the course of the next century the Carolingian Empire broke up. In the year A.D. 888 France, Germany and Italy emerged as distinct units, and the Pope was forced, in his determination to maintain the conception of the Empire, to invite the head of the strongest of these units to assume the Imperial crown.

Otto I of Germany had, like Charlemagne, fulfilled one necessary condition for the Imperial crown. He had acquired the throne of Italy. In A.D. 962 the Pope invited Otto I to renew once more the old Roman Empire. He was crowned by John XXII, and the Holy Roman Empire was at last launched on its career which did not terminate until A.D. 1806.

After the coronation of Otto, the relations between the Papacy and the Emperor remained friendly for about one hundred years, but ultimately degenerated into a feud which divided Europe into two camps. The quarrel about the right of investiture centred in the Papal claim that neither Emperor, king nor priest could give investiture of bishops. Ecclesiastical independence was the battle-ground in the eleventh century, and developed into a claim for ecclesiastical supremacy in the twelfth. Until 1059 the Emperor claimed to nominate the Pope, but after that date the Pope began to claim to nominate the Emperor.

Under the Hohenstaufen Emperors the first great chapter in the Holy Roman Empire came to an end. Frederick II aimed at the unification of Italy, a policy which threatened to bring the states of the Church under the rule of the Empire. The Pope summoned Charles of Anjou to his aid, with the result that when Rudolf of Habsburg succeeded to the Imperial crown the Emperor had lost all his rights in Italy save the titular rights in Lombardy, and was, in effect, only the head of a federation of German princes.

The Imperial crown was not hereditary, but elective. Under the ancient Roman Empire the principles of hereditary succession had never assumed any importance. The mediaeval Empire, instituted as it was by the Papacy, was naturally influenced by ecclesiastical preference for elective, rather than hereditary, succession. When Rudolf of Habsburg succeeded to the Imperial crown the electoral body consisted of three bishops and four great magnates. Since A.D. 962 the German king, elected by this body, was also *ipso facto* the Roman Emperor after coronation by the Pope. It was a matter of dispute whether the subse-quent coronation by the Pope was necessary to confirm the German king's right of succession to the Imperial crown.

The national character of the office gradually dis-appeared, and foreign potentates — among others Sigismund, who was virtually a Hungarian king—were often elected German kings and Emperors of Rome.

In theory, the Emperor was the representative of the Prince of Peace on earth, the supreme arbitrator in the quarrels between rival princes, and between princes and their peoples. He owed his position, not to hereditary right, still less to the will of the people, but to God, who used the electoral princes in the case of the Emperor much as He uses the College of Cardinals in the case of the Pope.

The Emperor claimed the right of creating kings, a right which was often admitted. Charles the Bold, the last Duke of Burgundy, for instance, desired to transform his dukedom into a kingdom, and it was from the Emperor that he sought permission to do so. The permission was refused, and he abandoned the project.

The Emperor was the head of the great Orders of chivalry, and the sovereigns of Europe long continued to address him in terms which admitted the inferiority of their own positions, and which yielded him the precedence which he claimed.

The Emperor normally went through three distinct coronations. At Aachen he was crowned king of the Franks, at Milan, king of Italy, and at Rome he received the double crown of the Roman Empire, *urbi et orbi*. These coronations were necessary, because the Imperial office, though it involved general suzerainty over all Christian kings, did not in itself carry the right to govern any particular kingdom. A feudal monarch might well be a duke or a count of lordships of which he was already, by virtue of his crown, the feudal superior. Similarly, the head of the feudal system was not necessarily the direct ruler of any particular territory, unless duly crowned as such.

Such were the Imperial pretensions of the Roman Emperor. His real powers bore little relation to his imposing claims. The chief object of the Electors was to prevent the king and Emperor from acquiring any real power. The Imperial dignity was thus often bestowed on some petty prince, and it was, indeed, Rudolf of Habsburg's comparative obscurity which rendered him a suitable candidate. As the dignity was not hereditary the Emperor tried to exploit his tenure of office by using his position to aggrandize his family. He treated the throne, as Lord Bryce remarks, as " a life tenant is apt to treat his estate, seeking only to make out of it the largest present profit."

The elective principle weakened the monarchy, for the successful candidate was forced to purchase his title by the sacrifice of rights which had belonged to his predecessors. The German king soon became virtually powerless, his authority parcelled out among a crowd of greedy and tyrannical nobles.

I have no space to trace the subsequent history of the Empire, but can only briefly refer to its final extinction. Napoleon tried to oust Francis II from his position as Holy Roman Emperor, but was anticipated by the proud Habsburg, who was resolved that no other should wear the crown which he was powerless to defend. On August 6th, 1806, he resigned the Imperial dignity. Thus perished the Holy Roman Empire, the oldest political institution in the Western world.

2. The Rise of the Habsburgs

The Imperial house of Habsburg with which the Holy Roman Empire was eventually identified, originated in a modest castle in Switzerland which can be reached in an hour's drive from Lucerne. On my first visit to the ancestral home of the Imperial family which at one time dominated Europe I took with me Mr. J. W. Gilbart-Smith's *The Cradle of the Habsburgs* and also the inimitable Baedeker. Mr. Gilbart-Smith recreates the past by writing " ye " for " the," and by a great deal of this kind of thing: " And, good reader, when thou art at Schinznach, make no doubt of it, straightway hie thee to the one hill which overlooketh the castle of Lenzburg; make no mistake on't and betake thyself to that mountain." Herr Karl Baedeker confines himself to the bleak facts: " The tower,

79 feet high, with walls 8 feet thick, is well preserved. The adjoining house is occupied by a farmer (rfmts.)."

At the beginning of the eleventh century the Count of Altenburg had lost his hawk, and a long search brought him to the summit of the Wülpelsburg, where he found his hawk and founded a house. The hawk, or to give it its German name, *Habicht*, gave its master not only a home but also a name, for the new stronghold was christened " Habisburg," which gradually became abbreviated to " Habsburg "—often written " Hapsburg."

It was Richenza, daughter of the Habsburg who built his stronghold on the Wülpelsburg hill, who started the Habsburg precedent of lucky marriages. She married Ulrich, Count von Lenzburg. The Lenzburg line became extinct in 1173, and by virtue of the above-mentioned marriage their possessions passed to the House of Habsburg, and another lucky marriage brought them the possessions of the House of Kyburg.

But it was left to Rudolf of Habsburg to force his way in 1273 to the Imperial throne itself.

Rudolf succeeded his father when the quarrel between the Papacy and the Emperor Friedrich of Germany was at its climax. The Emperor had been excommunicated, and Germany was divided between the supporters of Emperor and Pope. Rudolf, Count of Habsburg, remained faithful to the sovereign, thereby endangering his own possessions, for he risked excommunication, which would have provided the neighbouring nobles with the justification for taking possession of his lands.

At that time Switzerland was suffering from a plague of baronial brigands. Business was at a standstill, and the merchants of Basel and Lucerne and Geneva dared not trust their bales to the roads infested by bandits. The highroad from Basel towards Italy, for instance, was threatened by the robber stronghold of Regensberg, above Zürich.

Rudolf devoted all his energies to ridding Western Switzerland of these pests. He succeeded by a bold stratagem in capturing Regensberg and in razing it to the ground.

Germany, meanwhile (1254–1273), was suffering from the anarchy of an interregnum. The Electors could not, or would not, agree on a suitable candidate for the Imperial crown, and the Pope was becoming increasingly conscious of the evil results of weakening Germany. A Germany devastated by civil war could not, of course, contribute to the Papal revenue. There was no public law, no effective courts of justice, and no Emperor to embody the idea of legal government.

Rudolf may have taken the wrong side in the quarrel between Emperor and Pope, but the Pope was less impressed by Rudolf's politics than by his efficient record as a strong ruler. And a strong leader was needed before the Church lands in Germany could resume their ecclesiastical tributes.

The Pope, therefore, decided to force Rudolf on the Electors. The Electors, true to their principle of electing an obscure rather than a powerful prince, were quite prepared to accept this minor noble from the Swiss mountains rather than one of the greater of the German princes. And so by the irony of fate Rudolf was summoned from the siege of Basel, where he was busily engaged in waging war on the bishop, to assume in 1273 the Imperial crown as the Pope's nominee.

Rudolf, as German Emperor, purged Thuringia of robber barons as effectively as he had purged Western Switzerland. He lived on reasonably good terms with the Pope, even though he stoutly denied the Papal claims either to interfere in the election of the German sovereign or even to confer the Imperial dignity. He refused to cross the Alps to be crowned by the Pope, preferring to consolidate his position as German king rather than to assert his position as King of Italy or Emperor of Rome.

Rudolf was Landgrave of Alsace at the time of his
election. He also inherited through his mother a large
part of the lands of the extinct family of Zähringen, yet
another great Swiss family whose possessions had lapsed
through marriage to the Habsburgs. As German Emperor
he defeated and killed Ottocar II, King of Bohemia, and
invested his sons Albrecht and Rudolf with the duchies of
Austria and Styria, an event of supreme importance in the
history of the Habsburgs, for it was the first stage in trans-
ferring their authority from the Rhine to the Danube.

Rudolf's son Albrecht was also elected—in 1298—to the
Imperial crown, but was murdered by his nephew
Johannes, Duke of Austria, in 1308, and it was not until
Albrecht II of Habsburg became Emperor in 1438 that a
Habsburg again wore the Imperial crown. Thereafter all
the Emperors, with two exceptions, belonged to the House
of Habsburg.

The subsequent relations between the Habsburgs and
the Swiss Confederation will be described elsewhere in this
book. Here we need only summarise them briefly.
Leopold, Duke of Austria, who was defeated at Morgarten,
was the son of Albrecht I and a grandson of Rudolf. His
nephew, Duke Friedrich of Austria, lived for many years
at Lenzburg Castle. Another nephew of Leopold, called
Leopold III, was killed at Sempach.

In 1352 the Habsburg castle near Meggen on Lake
Lucerne was sacked by the Confederates, and in 1415 the
ancestral home of the Habsburgs on the Wülpelsburg was
sacked by the city of Berne. Nothing was left but the great
tower with its walls over eight feet thick, as they exist
to-day. The era of Habsburg domination over Switzerland
had definitely come to an end.

The old castle on the crest of the Wülpelsburg still
stands, a strangely unaffecting relic of the past. This
ancient stronghold is small and rather dreary, an unim-
pressive cradle for the race which furnished sixteen kings

to Germany, twenty-two to Austria, three to Portugal, eleven to Bohemia and Hungary, six to Spain, and but for Queen Mary's sterility, might have given England another. The best thing about the castle is the view.   In the plains below the Aar, the Limmat and the Reuss meet and mingle, and behind the low-lying hills of Aargau the distant gleam of the Oberland snows reveal a realm of adventure and romance which the Habsburgs never knew, and which was left to a later age to discover.

The castle, as Baedecker duly records, has been leased to a farmer, and it was his daughter who showed us over the castle and offered to introduce us into the banqueting hall (where " rfmts " were provided in bygone days) if we cared to pay an extra twopence, which we did.

After the first world war the ex-Empress Zita of Austria visited this castle with her children.   What thoughts were hers as she gazed out of the windows on to the hills from which the first Habsburg rode forth to seek his fortunes? The Imperial House whose descendants once dominated Europe has to-day less influence and power than the obscure Aargau noble who once occupied " the tower 79 feet high with walls 8 feet thick."

Chapter III

THE IMMORTAL MEADOW

1. The Rütli Legend

OF all lake journeys there is none lovelier than that from Lucerne to Flüelen. On my way to the Balkans, shortly after the outbreak of the war, I had dedicated a day to the lake, and the deciduous foliage of the forests seemed sadly symbolic of Europe's last hints of colour before the frost of the long winter of war. In 1945 I returned to Switzerland and as I embarked on the steamer at Lucerne I was joined by a happy pilgrimage of school children on their way to the immortal meadow of Rütli opposite Brunnen. It was on this meadow that the founders of Switzerland met on August 1st, 1291, to formulate the terms of an alliance, *Der Ewige Bund der drei Länder*, which proved to be the foundation charter of modern Switzerland. And it was to Rütli that General Guisan summoned the chiefs of the Swiss Army in 1940 when Switzerland was entirely hemmed in by the Axis Powers, to reaffirm their determination to blow up the Gotthard and Simplon tunnels in the event of an invasion and to retire to the Alpine *reduit* for a last stand. The Swiss determination to fight, if attacked, saved them from invasion.

The singing children left the steamer at Rütli and wandered up the little path to the immortal meadow. Barrés somewhere speaks of " places which are significant for the soul of man." Such places sometimes serve not only to recall the heroic past, but also to reinforce the political fashion of the moment. And as I watched the singing children disappear round a corner of the wooded path I wondered whether their conception of Rütli was the same as that which I had learned in my childhood from our Swiss nurse. Rütli, seen through her eyes, was a sacred meadow where simple mountain peasants, cut off from all commerce with the wicked world, swore a sacred oath to organise a revolution at once democratic and national, and thus laid the seeds of democratic Switzerland. Rütli was the opening act in a drama which culminated at Morgarten where peasants untutored in war defeated the professional armies of the hated Habsburg.

The facts of history lend no support to this sentimental legend. The nobility of the Forest Cantons played a leading rôle in the struggle for independence. The men of the Forest Cantons were not cut off from the world. On the contrary, one of the great arterial roads of mediaeval commerce led through the Forest Cantons to the Gotthard. The founders of Switzerland were conservatives concerned to defend existing rights rather than revolutionaries determined to create a new society. They were incapable of understanding what we mean either by Democracy or Nationalism. The Habsburgs were not capricious tyrants but shrewd calculating statesmen, who were ruthless perhaps in the exploitation of what they deemed to be their legal rights, but who were also influenced by the mediaeval reluctance to treat custom and established rights with contempt. Finally, the battle of Morgarten was won, not by simple peasants untutored in the art of war, but by competent professional soldiers who had acquired invaluable experience in foreign service.

2. Europe in the Thirteenth Century

We cannot begin to understand the Europe in which Switzerland was born until we realise the full implications of the religion which Europeans professed. Professed perhaps rather than practised, for Christians who make a serious attempt to practise what Christ preached have always been in the minority, but the Europe of the thirteenth century was none the less profoundly influenced by the basic Christian doctrine, the doctrine that God became man for our *salvation*. To the mediaeval Christian "salvation" had a precise significance. Christ died to save sinners from *Hell*. This world was a place where eternal issues were decided, a place of trial in which the ultimate fate of every individual soul was determined. In those days it would never have occurred to those who called themselves Christians that Christ was self-deceived when He warned His followers that He was destined to sit in judgment on mankind and that those who ignored His reiterated warnings might one day be numbered among the unrepentant sinners who would hear His stern judgment, without possibility of appeal, condemning them to eternal punishment. One need not be a Christian to realise that this doctrine, however unattractive, was a useful deterrent. "Thanks to a certain kind of progress," writes Aldous Huxley, "the rulers of the modern world no longer believe that they will be tortured everlastingly if they are wicked. The eschatological sanction which was one of the principal weapons in the hands of the prophets of past time has disappeared. This would not matter if moral had kept pace with intellectual 'progress.' But it has not. Twentieth-century rulers behave just as vilely as did rulers in the seventeenth or any other century. But unlike their predecessors they do not lie awake at nights wondering whether they are damned. If Marie de Medici had enjoyed the advantages of a modern education Father Joseph would have thundered in vain and Angers would have been sacked."

It is because modern tyrants no longer fear supernatural sanctions that their brutality is wholly unrestrained and their signature at the bottom of treaties means nothing. Barbarossa might expel the Pope from Rome and send him wandering a helpless suitor through all the courts of

Europe but Barbarossa believed in Hell and he ended by doing obeisance in the Piazza of St. Mark's, Venice, to an old man armed only with powers which are not of this world. Henry II exclaimed, " Who will rid me of this pestilent priest? " and Mussolini exclaimed, in effect, " Who will rid me of this pestilent politician? " and Henry II ended by flogging himself in penitence at the tomb of St. Thomas à Becket, but Mussolini did not flog himself at the grave of Matteoti.

The men of the Forest Cantons, as we shall see, won their independence by playing off the distant Emperor against their Habsburg neighbours. Imperial protection was of little value either in terms of military or economic assistance. The Emperor was too far away to intervene effectively. If the Habsburgs had recognised no reality transcending that of power politics, the Forest Cantons would have been as helpless as the Russian satellite states are to-day, but in an age in which all valid authority was deemed to be derived from God, the authority of the Emperor rested on other foundations than military power, for there was still an immense, if often unwilling, respect for the authority of the Emperor as the supreme political authority in the Christian world. Similarly even those who took up arms against the Pope never questioned his supreme authority in the domain of Religion, and because men believed in supernatural sanctions they did not lightly disregard such solemn obligations as they had contracted, and though treaties were sometimes broken they were more often observed, for even tyrants hesitated to treat treaties as scraps of paper or customary rights as of no account. The Habsburgs were very far from being the capricious tyrants of Schiller's play. Schiller had no clue to the legalism of a period in history when wars, as Bishop Stubbs insisted, were often fought on a point of right, wars of interest being an innovation of the Renaissance. The Habsburg march to power was in accordance with mediaeval conceptions of legality. They inherited certain rights, purchased others and increased their territory by a series of careful marriages. *Tu felix Austria nube*. There were occasional abuses of power by their functionaries, but the first blatant breach with legality in the struggles which led to Swiss independence was committed, not by the Habsburgs, but by the marauding band of Schwyz who in 1314 attacked the Abbey of Einsiedeln, and thus provoked what the Habsburgs no doubt regarded as a mere punitive expedition. Had Morgarten been a victory for the Habsburgs, contemporary public opinion would have felt as little sympathy for the men of the Forest Cantons as England felt for the Sudanese who were crushed in the campaign the primary object of which was to avenge the murder of General Gordon.

The thirteenth century was not only an age of great creative activity, the century of cathedral building, of the *Summa Theologica* and Dante's *Divine Comedy*. It was also a century of political transition. In the course of four centuries Feudalism had lost many of its beneficial characteristics. The Feudal system was valued in its best period for much the same reasons that an effective police force is valued to-day. The Emperor, source of all temporal power, had delegated to the great Feudal nobles the duty of maintaining law and order in their territories. But gradually the concept of social function had been transformed into a concept of social privilege. Absenteeism and exclusiveness, the endemic vices of a decadent aristocracy, rendered Feudalism less and less acceptable not only to the common people but also to the rising class of the commercial bourgeoisie, who tolerated with ever-growing impatience the arbitrary demands of feudal lords. The respect which great nobles had enjoyed as the guardians of order was no longer accorded to rulers who exacted exorbitant fees for protection and demanded vexatious dues from all merchandise which passed through their territories. Throughout Europe trading communities concentrated on liberating themselves from a feudal class which had outlived its usefulness. The Lombard communities secured their liberties from Frederic as early as 1183, and in 1215, the year of Magna Carta, Cologne and Strasbourg became free towns and their example was followed by Basel in 1264, by St. Gall in 1272 and by Solothurn in 1280.

Our Victorian forebears were convinced that nationalism would decline as means of communication improved, but there is no evidence that the aeroplane has strengthened the ties of friendship between peoples separated by journeys of a few hours compared to the many weeks which were spent on similar journeys in the coaching days. There was far more genuine internationalism in mediaeval than in modern Europe and far fewer obstacles to travel even though travel was far more laborious and expensive than it is to-day.

The influence of local patriotism was never stronger than in the Middle Ages. It was this devotion to the political cell, the small urban or agricultural community, that was the seed from which Switzerland was born, but nationalism, as we now know it, was unknown until the fifteenth century. The allegiance which a thirteenth-century European owed to his local community or his feudal lord in no way conflicted with his loyalty to Christendom, as represented by the Pope in the religious and by the Emperor in the temporal sphere. In those days the unity of Christendom was a reality, and Internationalism was a reality because the unity of Christendom was the basic postulate of all political thought.

In the thirteenth century nobles travelled from court to court, from tourney to tourney, and the " clerks," or the educated classes, most of whom were in orders, wandered freely from one university to another. What Czech would to-day obtain permission to study at Oxford?

Educated men could exchange ideas in Latin, and some at least of the secular aristocracy were men of taste and wide reading, familiar with the new literature in the vulgar tongues, German, Italian or French as the case might be. The rising class of merchants did business with all Europe and even with the Orient, and the aristocracy and merchants who lived on the greater commercial routes from Flanders and Germany to Italy, *via* the Alpine passes, were in constant touch with the ferment of new ideas which was slowly transforming Europe. The minor nobility of the Forest Cantons were relatively provincial in their outlook compared to the great feudal dignitaries, and moreover they lacked those international contacts which are the accompaniment of great wealth, but the younger scions of the leading families were critical of the accepted traditions, and influenced by the movements of commerce and of thought which made themselves felt when the shortening of the St. Gotthard route imparted a new and decisive importance to the Forest Cantons.

3. The Importance of the St. Gotthard Pass

The St. Gotthard was not " opened " in the twelfth century, as every Swiss history that I have read implies. The pass was known in Roman times. But, some time between 1180 and 1190, the St. Gotthard route was *shortened* by rendering the passage of the Schöllenen Gorge practicable and from that moment the St. Gotthard replaced the Lukmanier as the best route from Flanders and Germany into Italy. The new importance of the St. Gotthard was reflected in the status of the Forest Cantons. The Habsburgs were determined to control the approach to the St. Gotthard, the Hohenstaufen Emperors were equally convinced that the relative independence of the Forest Cantons was of primary importance to them, since they could not afford to allow the Habsburgs to cut

them off from the main approach to Italy. The Forest
Cantons, as we shall see, won their independence by
playing off the Habsburgs against the Emperor. Even
when a Habsburg was himself Emperor the Forest Cantons
never allowed the Habsburgs to confuse the rights which
they enjoyed *qua* Emperor with the rights which they
enjoyed *qua* Habsburg.

It is impossible to exaggerate the importance of the
St. Gotthard in the struggle for independence. The
increasing traffic across this pass transformed many of the
men of Uri from agriculturists into traders. Many of
them made a living by providing mules or acting as guides
across the pass. Moreover, the traffic across the pass
exposed the Forest Cantons to the new wind of freedom
which was blowing from Italy, where the communes were
fighting an unsuccessful war of liberation against the
Emperor. The pious legend according to which the men
of the Forest Cantons had preserved their passion for
liberty thanks to their remoteness from the great world is
the exact reverse of the truth. On the contrary, as the
Swiss historian William Martin points out, it was at the
moment that this remoteness ceased that movement for
independence began.

4. The Strategy of the Forest Cantons

The first object of the Forest Cantons was to secure
Reichsunmittelbarkeit, that is to say to place themselves under
the immediate lordship of the Emperor. They preferred
the rule of the Emperor to the rule of the Habsburgs for
many reasons, of which the most important was that they
preferred the remote control of the Emperor to the control
of the Habsburg on the door step. In the thirteenth
century the tax collector was not the revered and beloved
official that he is to-day, and taxes were not paid with that
cheerful readiness which is normal in our progressive age.
The Emperor was a long way off, and far less efficient as a

tax collector than the Habsburgs. To be directly subject to the Emperor was a status as near to actual independence as the Forest Cantons could ever hope to achieve. Consequently the Urners (as the men of Uri were called) were dismayed when the Hohenstaufen Emperor mortgaged Uri to the Habsburgs to cover the costs of his Italian campaign. This was a normal method of raising money, and as the Emperor was chronically short of cash such mortgages were never redeemed. Rheinfelden, Murten, Laupen and the Haslital, for instance, were lost for ever to the Empire once they were mortgaged.

The Urners, on the other hand, were made of sterner stuff. By severe taxation they raised the necessary sum to pay off the mortgage and thus to place themselves again under the immediate rule of the Emperor. Never has a creditor accepted payment with a worse grace than the Habsburgs who had advanced the money on mortgage with the firm intention of establishing permanent control over the vital St. Gotthard route. On May 26th, 1231, Heinrich VII set seal to a solemn declaration that Uri would never again be mortgaged, and confirmed the Urners in their rights. Little did this Hohenstaufen monarch realise that he had laid the secure foundation of the first Swiss Canton. In 1239 the Emperor was excommunicated. In the following year Rudolf the Silent, uncle of the Rudolf who was to be elected Emperor in 1273, in contrast to other branches of the Habsburg family, deserted the Emperor for the Pope.

Now the men of Schwyz and Obwalden* were pious Catholics who accepted without question the Pope as the spiritual head of Christendom, but were inhibited by no religious scruples from allying themselves with the Emperor against the Pope in his function as the temporal ruler of the Papal States. When their Habsburg overlord changed

* The Canton of Unterwalden is divided into two half Cantons, Obwalden or Upper-Walden, and Nidwalden or Lower-Walden.

sides they registered their disapproval by sacking the Habsburg strongholds in their domains. Everybody has heard of Morgarten and Sempach, but these local risings, the first in which the Forest Cantons took up arms to assert their independence, are all but forgotten. After this lively demonstration they sent a deputation to Italy where the Hohenstaufen Emperor Friedrich II was besieging Faenza, and obtained from him a solemn declaration of imperial protection *als freie Leute* (as free men).

In 1242, Rudolf the Silent changed sides once again and declared himself once more a faithful vassal of the Emperor. This was very annoying to the faithful vassals in Schwyz and Obwalden, for their policy was based on the slogan : " For the Emperor against his faithless Vassals."

From 1254 to 1273 there was no Emperor, and the great interregnum ended with the election of Rudolf of Habsburg, nephew of Rudolf the Silent. Now that a Habsburg was Emperor, the men of the Forest Cantons were no longer able to play off the Emperor against the Habsburgs. They were wise enough to recognise the Habsburg as their Emperor but they stubbornly refused to concede to Rudolf, as Habsburg, any rights of stewardship in their cantons.

Rudolf refused to recognise the charter of Faenza, but he promised that no citizen of the Forest Cantons should be judged except by himself or his sons or a Landammann born and bred in the Forest Cantons. As, however, he ruled as Emperor over half of Europe, both he and his sons were too busy to act as local J.P.s in remote mountain valleys. He aggravated the offence by sending foreign bailiffs, some of whom were not of free birth, a fact which incensed class-conscious Schwyz. In those days a marriage between a noble and a free peasant was not regarded as a mesalliance, but the children born of a marriage between a free and unfree peasant had servile status. The pious legend which attributes the foundation of Switzerland to democratic egalitarians in revolt against a hierarchical society is not easy to reconcile with the fact that one of the grievances which provoked the revolt was that the free men of the Forest Cantons bitterly resented being subjected to bailiffs of low birth.

On July 15th, 1291, Rudolf of Habsburg, Roman Emperor and German King, died. As the Imperial throne was not hereditary, the Habsburg agents at once attempted to establish on a firm basis the Habsburg rights in the Forest Cantons. The men of the Forest Cantons were even less dilatory in taking every possible step to guard their independence.

5. William Tell—History or Legend?

Let me begin with the traditional story of William Tell, the story which forms the basis of Schiller's play and Rossini's opera.

Gessler, the Habsburg Landvogt, caused a pole to be set up in the market place of Altdorf and his hat to be placed on the pole as a token of Habsburg ascendancy. William Tell passed through the market place without the least sign of respect to Gessler's hat, and was promptly arrested, but offered his freedom if he could shoot an apple placed on his son's head. Tell, a famous marksman, pierced the apple in two, but Gessler noticed that he had carefully placed a second arrow in his quiver, and Tell admitted that he would have used this arrow to shoot Gessler had he killed his son. He was promptly arrested, and forced on to a boat which had no sooner left the shore than a terrible storm came down on the lake and threatened them with shipwreck. Tell was set free from the ropes which bound him on the understanding that he would steer the boat, but no sooner had the boat approached a rocky promontory than Tell leapt to safety and escaped. He shortly afterwards killed Gessler in an ambush on the Hohle Gasse near Küssnacht.

So much for the William Tell of tradition. It is probable

that the anonymous hero subsequently called Tell was in fact a member of the inner circle of conspirators whose chief was Stauffacher. Stauffacher was one of the signatories of the famous Ewige Bund of Rütli, and the Gessler of legend was really called Tillendorf. " A sort of triumphant shriek," wrote Ruskin, " like all the railway whistles going off at Clapham Junction, has gone up from the fooldom of Christendom at the destruction of the myth of William Tell." Ruskin was right and the " fooldom " was wrong, for the Tell story is not wholly mythical. There is to-day far more respect among historians for tradition than was fashionable in the nineteenth century, for the modern historians are more scientific than their predecessors and realise that most traditions are founded on fact. The distinguished Swiss historian, Dr. Karl Meyer of Zürich, is convinced that the basis of the Tell legend is historical. Here is a summary of the case which he presents in his book *Die Freiheitskampf der Eidgenössischen Bundesgründer* (pp. 40 to 41).

The moment that it was realised that Rudolf's days were numbered, the Swabian knight Tillendorf, Obervogt of Kiburg, hurried to Uri in order to protect the Habsburg interests.

Tillendorf, an imperial judge in Uri, like the Gessler of tradition, caused a pole to be set up in the market place of Altdorf and his own hat to be placed on the pole as a token of Habsburg ascendancy. It is probable that somebody closely associated with the inner ring of Stauffacher's conspiracy treated this hat with contempt as he passed through the market place, and, if so, he may well have received a savage sentence and escaped, as did Tell, by leaping ashore from the boat which was carrying him into captivity. This episode is supposed to have taken place near the scene of the second of Tell's chapels. According to tradition, William Tell killed Gessler in an ambush near Küssnacht and the first of Tell's chapels, in the Hohle Gasse near Küssnacht, commemorates this incident. Now it is probable that long before the present chapel was built, a chapel was erected at this point by Albrecht of Habsburg, in memory not of the rebel of Uri but of the man he killed. And that man's name was not Gessler but Tillendorf. Just as Hitler would never have allowed a chapel to be erected to the memory of a Czech who had killed one of his Gauleiters, so no chapel could have been erected during the era of Habsburg domination in honour of a rebel who had assassinated a Habsburg " Vogt." Dr. Karl Meyer believes that a chapel was erected by the Habsburgs for the repose of the soul of Tillendorf, and that as the years passed this name, Tillendorf, became confused with the word " Tellen," and the Tillendorf chapel became the Tellenkapelle, and that after the liberation of Schwyz it gradually came to be believed that the Tillendorf chapel had been built, not as the memorial to a Habsburg Vogt, but as a memorial to the liberator of Uri, with the result that the latter was assumed to have been called Tell. Schiller, following local tradition, calls his tyrant Gessler, but the real Gessler was a subordinate of Tillendorf's, the Untervogt in Schwyz. As late as 1511 it was well known in Uri that the Landvogt who crowned the pole in the market place of Altdorf with his hat was not called Gessler.

6. August 1st, 1291

The free men of the Forest Cantons were undismayed by Tillendorf's attempts to cow them into submission. On the contrary, they lost no time in proving that they were as good men as their grandfathers who had sacked the Habsburg strongholds in Schwyz and Obwalden, as the unfortunate owners of Habsburg castles in Uri soon discovered.

On August 1st, 1291, representatives of Uri, Schwyz and Unterwalden met on the meadow of Rütli and signed

Der Ewige Bund der drei Länder (the everlasting alliance of the three lands). An important clause in this alliance was a joint declaration that they would admit no foreign judge to their valleys.

The signatories were neither democrats, in the modern sense of the term, nor the conscious founders of a new State. On this point there is agreement between two brilliant historians who approach the past from different poles of political philosophy. Professor Gonzague de Reynold, a Catholic, a Patrician and an extreme Conservative, and Herr Robert Grimm, a Socialist member of the Swiss Nationalrat, and imprisoned for revolutionary activities at the end of the first world war, are both agreed that the men who laid the foundations of modern Switzerland accepted, as Herr Grimm insists, " the social structure as self-evident and beyond criticism." The terms of the alliance insist by implication on the duty of every man to obey his master—*seinem Herrn nach Gebühr gehorsam zu sein und zu dienen.* It was essentially a Conservative document uninfluenced by any desire to secure new rights or to obliterate existing class distinctions.

" They confined themselves," writes Herr Grimm, " to the safeguarding of inherited rights and defended themselves only against *new* burdens and restrictions."

Herr Grimm remarks that every Swiss liberation movement has sought its inspiration in the past. The men of Uri invoked ancient rights and charters, " as if their ideal was to be sought not in the future but recovered from the past."*

Many of those who, in the attempt to defend existing rights, were in fact responsible for revolutionary changes belonged to the minor nobility, such as the Attinghausen and the Silenen families. Some of the leaders were free peasants who owned great properties. Revolutions are

* *Geschichte der Schweiz in ihren Klassenkampfen.* This history was written while Herr Grimm was a political prisoner.

D

not made by Gallup Polls, but by an *élite*. The men of the Forest Cantons succeeded mainly because the resistance to the Habsburgs was organised by a small group of highly intelligent leaders who played such cards as they possessed with consummate skill and who missed no opportunity provided by rivalries between Pope and Emperor, or between Emperor and Habsburg.

But the political genius of the *élite* which determined the policy of the Forest Cantons would have availed little had the rank and file been less disciplined and less devoted to their traditions. The social structure of the Forest Cantons provided the perfect matrix for liberation. The ordeal which tested them would have proved too exacting for a society which was not both anchored in tradition, and also prepared for the great experiment of independence. A society which is too conservative stagnates, and a society which is too radical disintegrates. The ideal State, as Burke remarked, " is a partnership not only between those who are living but also between those who are dead and those who are to be born," and the emancipation of the Forest Cantons vindicates the wisdom of another of Burke's famous sayings, " A people will not look forward to posterity who never looked back to their ancestors."

Chapter IV

THE DECISIVE BATTLES

IN 1298 a Habsburg Duke was once again elected Roman Emperor, a serious blow to the men of the Forest Cantons, not only because their traditional policy was to play off the Emperor against the Habsburgs, but also because this particular Duke Albrecht had for years been attempting to subdue the Forest Cantons by means of an economic blockade both by land and lake. No more striking evidence of their passionate love of freedom can be cited than the fact that the destruction of their trade and the spectre of hunger could not force them to surrender. Fortunately for the Forest Cantons, Albrecht was murdered on May 1st, 1308, and fortunately for the cause of Swiss freedom no Habsburg again secured undisputed election to the Imperial throne until 1438. Henry VII of Luxemburg, who succeeded to the Habsburgs, died in Italy in 1313, and Leopold, Duke of Habsburg, exploited all his connections and all his influence in the attempt to secure for his elder brother, Frederic, the good will of the Electors. He enjoyed a partial and, as events proved, a temporary success, for Frederic was elected Emperor on October 19th, 1314, but only by a minority of the Electors. The remainder proceeded to declare that Ludwig of Bavaria, a bitter enemy of the Habsburgs, was the rightful Emperor. Whereupon a dynastic war broke out, which lasted for sixteen years, and did not end in victory for the Habsburg claimant. The Forest Cantons, of course, gave their full support to the Bavarian.

Meanwhile the Forest Cantons were giving ever-increasing scandal to the Habsburgs by their democratic tendencies. I use the words " democratic " and " democracy " for want of better terms to describe a form of government which resembles modern democracies in the mechanics of election and in little else. It is indeed difficult to avoid the clichés of modern political shibboleths in describing the Landesgemeinde, the first of which met in Schwyz in 1295. The Landesgemeinde endures to this day in some Cantons, and both in its ancient and in its present form is the simplest and most thorough expression of democracy in action. All the adult citizens of the Canton assemble together to elect officers and to pass laws. It is, indeed, the government of the whole people by the whole people, and not merely by the representatives of the people. At this first historic meeting a law was passed which laid the foundation of modern Switzerland. The assembled peoples of Schwyz agreed that it should be forbidden to sell land either to the monasteries or to strangers outside the valley. This decree established for all time the principle of peasant proprietorship, and marked the first dawn of revolt against absentee landlords, and against the monopoly of land by ecclesiastical corporations.

The immediate cause which provoked the Habsburgs to organise a punitive expedition for the chastisement of the Forest Cantons was the sacking of the great Benedictine Monastery of Einsiedeln by the men of Schwyz. The boundaries between Schwyz and the territory subject to the Monastery of Einsiedeln had never been exactly defined and the Habsburg blockade of the Forest Cantons weakened their respect for territorial boundaries. According to Ruskin, the men of Schwyz "sustained with tranquillity the excommunication of Abbots who wanted to feed their cattle on other people's fields." The truth is that the Schwyzois were forced by economic necessity to feed their cattle on the Abbots' fields. I do not know how Ruskin defined "tranquillity," but certainly Schwyzois tranquillity was not first cousin to appeasement. What actually happened was that the Schwyzois mobilised on the Feast of the Epiphany in 1314, marched on Einsiedeln, sacked the Monastery and took the monks back to Schwyz, where they were imprisoned for several days. As the Monastery had been placed under the direct protection of the Habsburgs, this display of " tranquillity " finally convinced the Habsburgs that nothing but a full-scale punitive expedition could solve the problem of the Forest Cantons. Like Hitler, the Habsburgs felt that their patience was exhausted. For a quarter of a century these mountain men had befriended all their enemies, had not concealed their enthusiastic support and approval of the assassins of Albrecht, and the time had come to teach them a lesson.

Meanwhile the Forest Cantons were not passively awaiting the Habsburg onslaught. They numbered among their warriors many who had served for years in foreign wars, particularly under the Hohenstaufens. There is no basis whatsoever for the pious legend which represents them as simple mountain peasants untutored in the art of war. Their preparations had begun as early as 1290, and by the time the punitive expedition left Zug the land approach through Arth was already sealed off by a fence of palisades which stretched from the Rigi to the Rüfiberg. A second line of defence had been constructed near the Enge of Oberarth. The Renggpass and the Brünig had also been fortified. The Habsburgs enjoyed a virtual command of the lake, but the ports of Brunnen and Buochs were fortified and the Forest Cantons did not confine themselves to passive defence. By a series of spirited sorties on the lake against the Habsburg ports they maintained an active war of nerves.

In the autumn of 1315, Duke Leopold of Austria mobilised his army in Aargau. " The men of his army," writes a contemporary chronicler, Joannes Vitoduranus, " came together with one purpose—utterly to subdue and humiliate those peasants who were surrounded with mountains as with walls."

Leopold's plan was to march on Schwyz over the low Sattel Pass across the Morgarten ridge, a few miles north of Schwyz. Morgarten is not a dizzy mountain pass, but a gentle depression in an undulating ridge of hills. The scenery has none of the grandeur of the authentic Alps, but has its own quiet charm, all the more persuasive by contrast with the more rugged glories of the mountains which disappear from view as one crosses the low-lying hills which open out on to the gentler beauties of the Aegeri Lake.*

On November 15th, 1315, the Duke and his knights approached the pass of Morgarten which the men of the Forest Cantons had deliberately left undefended, hoping to lure the Habsburgs into a trap. The Duke meanwhile had created a diversion by an attack on Stansstad in the Canton of Unterwalden, from which reinforcements had been sent to the Confederates at the battle of Morgarten. Lucerne, at that time, had not joined the Swiss Confederates, and was still in alliance with Austria, and in later days she must have recalled with shame the fact that she sent troops to attack the young Confederation at Stansstad, and also attempted to land at Buochs in order to create a diversion in Austria's favour. The women of Buochs, in the absence of their menfolk, who were fighting at Morgarten, beat off the invaders, and in recognition of their gallantry obtained the right, which they still enjoy, of approaching the Communion rail before the other sex. At Stansstad the market-boat of Uri came to the rescue. Eventually the Lucerne flagship was put out of action by a millstone launched from the watchtower, a primitive form of aerial bomb.

Meanwhile the men of Schwyz, reinforced by men from Uri and Unterwalden, posted themselves on the Sattel Pass, unseen and unsuspected by the Austrian knights who rode gaily to their doom along the shores of Lake Aegeri.

* Morgarten is easily reached in an afternoon's motor run from Lucerne. A delightful expedition is to combine a visit to Morgarten and Einsiedeln, returning to Lucerne via Brunnen.

Their burnished armour glittered in the morning light, and against the sombre greens of the forest their fluttering pennons made a brave show. They laughed and jested, and inquired anxiously whether their attendants had provided themselves with sufficient rope to lead back the captured cattle. They were much amused by the Duke's fool who, when asked what he thought of the plan of invasion, replied:—"You have all taken counsel how best to get into the country, but have given no explanation of how you are going to get out again."

They climbed slowly, in single file, toward the pass, their line of battle necessarily broken. Near the top of the pass the leaders halted and looked anxiously up toward the steep hillsides, down which a few stray rocks and pebbles had just fallen. Suddenly an avalanche of huge boulders and tree-trunks crashed down the slopes. The narrow pass of Morgarten was turned into a death-trap—a desperate struggling confusion of men and horses. And then came the human avalanche, an irresistible torrent of peasants swinging their deadly halberds and scythes. Beneath these rude weapons the chivalry of the Empire fell. Some died on the spot, others were driven into the lake, while others were killed by falling boulders. The rout was complete, but let us hope that the Duke's fool, at least, escaped.

Morgarten was perhaps the first battle of the Middle Ages in which an army of mounted knights was beaten by peasants on foot.

On December 9th, 1315, the Confederates renewed their first league at the village of Brunnen, and three years later the Dukes of Austria decided to make peace with them.

The Confederation rapidly expanded. Lucerne was naturally the first to join. Zürich, Glarus, Zug, and Berne all followed the example of Lucerne in the course of the following year. The growth in strength of the young Confederation was, of course, viewed with alarm by Austria, and in 1386, Duke Leopold III, nephew of the Leopold who was defeated at Morgarten, mobilised a large army, the immediate object of which was to chastise Lucerne. The Duke's army was utterly defeated, and the Duke himself lost his life on the battlefield of Sempach, ten miles from Lucerne. It was in this battle that Arnold von Winkelried gathered the Austrian spears in his bosom in order to force a breach in the enemy's ranks by which his countrymen could enter. There is some reason to suppose that this story is not altogether legendary, for a man of that name was certainly living in Stans at the time of the battle, and as Stans fought on the Confederates' side, it is at least probable that Arnold von Winkelried fought with them.

Two years later, in 1388, Austria suffered her third defeat in an attempt to reduce the rebellious peasants of Glarus. Once again they were heavily routed, this time at Näfels, at the north end of the Linthal. After various attempts to seduce Zürich from the Confederation, Austria bowed to the inevitable, and signed a treaty of peace. From this time forward the young Confederation, though still within the Empire, was no longer of it. The Germans began to speak of the Cantons which formed this Confederation as *Die Schweiz*, after Schwyz. The battles of Morgarten, Sempach, and Näfels planted the seeds of modern Switzerland. The Cantons which resisted the Habsburgs began as a league of small states within the Empire and emerged a nation. Their success was the more susprising because at that very time the liberties so gallantly defended on the shores of the Lake of Lucerne were being trampled underfoot in Germany. In Germany the monarchical principle was in the ascendant, and the Leagues of the Swabian cities and of the Rhine cities were being crushed. In Switzerland, on the other hand, the principles of a primitive democracy were established on an enduring foundation.

Chapter V

THE CENTRAL CANTONS AND THE REFORMATION

1. Marignano and Zwingli

AT the end of the fifteenth century the Swiss had extended their conquests south of the St. Gotthard Pass. They were in possession of the Levantina, and they coveted Bellinzona, the key of the St. Gotthard. Louis XII had promised them Bellinzona in return for their help in conquering the Duchy of Milan, and when the King failed to keep his promise, the Swiss not only seized Bellinzona but laid siege to Arona which Louis was forced to yield, and conquered the Val Blénio. They subsequently joined the coalition which Pope Julius II had formed against France, and indeed supplied the greater part of its military strength. On June 14th, 1512, the Swiss were victorious at Pavia, and on June 20th they entered Milan. At the end of the month the Swiss had occupied Domodossola, Locarno, Lugano and Mendrisio while their allies of the Grisons, not yet formally citizens of the Swiss Confederation, had seized the valley of the Adda, and the seignories of Bormio and Chiavanna which they were to retain until 1797. Wherever the Swiss succeeded in expelling the French they were welcomed as liberators.

In 1513 the King of France made a new attempt to regain Milan, but was defeated at Novarra.

The year 1513 marked the peak of Swiss military power and prestige. They not only defeated the French in Italy, but they took the offensive against the French in France itself, entered Burgundy, laid siege to Dijon, and finally made peace on extremely favourable terms. Their career of conquest was brought to an end on September 14th, 1515, when Francis I, who succeeded Louis XII, defeated the Swiss near Milan, a defeat which is the theme of one of Hodler's most famous paintings. The battle of Marignano was of decisive importance in the history of Switzerland for two reasons. This defeat virtually brought to an end the expansionist policy of Switzerland, but the desperate courage of the Swiss made such a deep impression on Francis I that within a year he had signed a treaty with them which was to remain in force until the French Revolution, and which, as we shall see in a later chapter, was perhaps the most important of all factors in the preservation of Swiss independence.

Finally, the defeat of the Swiss at Marignano was of decisive importance in precipitating the Swiss Protestant Reformation. Swiss ambitions to become a great power might have survived Marignano but for the fact that Marignano completed the transformation of a young Catholic military chaplain whose name was Zwingli into an isolationist and a Protestant Reformer. It was, indeed, the Reformation, with its paralysing effect on Swiss unity, and therefore on Swiss foreign policy, which deprived the Swiss for good or for evil of all hope of continuing their great rôle on the European stage.

Ulrich Zwingli was born on January 1st, 1484, at Wildhaus in the Canton of St. Gall, and was appointed parish priest of Glarus in 1506. As army chaplain he accompanied the Swiss troops into Italy and was present at the defeat of Marignano. His experiences as a military chaplain convinced him that the Swiss should retire within their own frontiers and be content with the simple life of a country with no ambition to play a great part in foreign affairs. In 1518 he was elected Rector of the Minster at Zürich where his career as a Protestant Reformer began. He began as a critic of the celibacy of the clergy. He and ten other priests petitioned the Bishop of Constance to permit their marriage. " Your honourable wisdom," Zwingli wrote, " has already witnessed the shameful and disgraceful life we have led with women, thereby giving grievous scandal to everybody." The petition was refused, and it was not until 1524, after his final breach with Rome, that Zwingli legalised his relations with Anne Reinhard.

His bitter attacks on the practice of sending Swiss to serve in foreign armies appealed, as we shall see in a later chapter, to the citizens of Zürich who could obtain the necessary foreign currency by trade, but not to the rural Cantons which balanced their budgets by means of remittances sent home by the Swiss in foreign service. Zürich, on the other hand, owed its prosperity to the fact that it was the crossroads of two great trade routes, Germany to Italy across the St. Gotthard, and from Austria into France via the Arlberg Pass. It is, incidentally, interesting to note that the Reformation triumphed in Zürich as the result of an alliance between intellectuals and the proletariat, an alliance identical with that which in more modern times brought about the triumph of Socialism and Communism in urban centres.

Zwingli's strategy as a Reformer, determined to conquer Switzerland for the Reformation, was to demand what he called " Liberty of preaching." Of course neither Zwingli nor his Catholic opponents maintained that people should be free to practise the religion which they preferred. The only point at issue between Zwingli and the Catholics was whether every parish should be free to hear the case for the Reformation, and then to decide by a majority vote whether or no to adopt the Reformation doctrines. Zwingli never concealed his intention that the majority decision, if favourable to Protestantism, should be binding on the minority. Be it noted that neither Zwingli nor Zürich had the least intention of inviting Catholic preachers to put their case before the parishes which had adopted the Reformation. He had no more intention than Stalin has of offering his opponents those propaganda facilities in his territory which he claims in theirs.

2. The Religious Wars

The relations between Zürich and Zwingli were consequently strained, but the Protestant Cantons, other than Zürich, did not want war, and Berne imposed herself as mediator on the unwilling Zwingli, with the result that a peace was concluded on February 16th, 1529, in which Zwingli could only obtain the " liberty of preaching " in the subject bailiwicks, the control of which was jointly shared by Zürich and the Catholic Cantons. It is said that the armies actually met at Kappel, on the frontier between Catholic Zug and Zürich, but that no fighting took place. The Catholics had milk but no bread, and they placed the bowl of milk on the frontier between Zürich and Zug. The Zürich men turned up with loaves and presently Protestants and Catholics were merrily consuming the Milchsuppe together, an incident famous in Swiss history as the Kappel Milchsuppe.

" This peace," exclaimed Zwingli, " is a war." Zwingli had quarrelled with Luther and was having difficulties with important members of the Zürich Council. Zwingli, as the Genevese historian William Martin remarks, wanted a war to divert attention from the conflicts in which he was involved, and then failed to organise it properly. Zürich repeated the tactics of the Habsburgs and blockaded the Catholic Cantons. Menaced by starvation, they were forced to attack as a measure of self-defence. In two decisive battles, at Kappel on October 11th and at Gubel on October 23rd, 1531, the Catholics gained a decisive victory, a victory but for which the whole of Switzerland might have been lost to the Catholics. Zwingli was killed on October 11th before Kappel.

On November 20th a peace was signed. The Catholics were moderate in their demands. Their restraint was a concession to expediency rather than to principle, for they did not want to risk provoking Protestant Berne into an overt defence of Protestant interests. They had no need to be anything but moderate for the prestige which they gained by their victory was of decisive importance in the history of Switzerland. The momentum of the Swiss Reformation had been definitely brought to a standstill. The period of advance which had lasted for a quarter of a century had ended, and the advance was never renewed. On the contrary the Catholics regained lost ground at Rapperswyl, Sargans, Toggenburg and in the Rhine valley.

Where moderation was not imposed by expediency the Catholics proved no more merciful in their hour of victory than the Protestants where the situation was reversed. The little Protestant community of Locarno was brutally dispersed with the result that the Pestalozzis, Orellis and Muralts took refuge in Zürich. The Protestant ancestor of a famous Swiss Minister to the Court of St. James, Mr. Paravacini, left Locarno for Basel at the time of this persecution.

3. The Precarious Equilibrium

The political equilibrium established by this peace was precarious, for the bare majority (7 to 6) which the Catholic Cantons enjoyed in the Diet did not correspond to the relative economic strength or population of the two parties. Mr. R. H. Tawney's thesis that there is a close connection between the rise of Protestantism and the rise of capitalism finds much support in Switzerland where the Catholics lost the great industrial centres and were only strong in the country districts, mountain valleys and lesser towns. The same contrast is broadly true of modern Switzerland, and it is always safe to offer odds on that a big factory in a small Catholic town, Zug, for instance, has been built by Protestant money. There is a constant tendency for towns to drain the countryside and for this reason the bare majority which the Catholic Cantons commanded in the Diet did not represent a majority of the population, but the precarious balance between the two parties was maintained because the only alternative was the disruption of Switzerland. The doctrine of perpetual neutrality is the direct consequence of Swiss disunity. A divided country cannot afford foreign adventures.

4. Foreign Alliances

That the Swiss were not yet wholly reconciled to neutrality was made clear in 1536 when the spirit of expansionist adventure which had once carried the Swiss into northern Italy to the gates of Milan and beyond, flared up for the last time in a war of unashamed aggression against the Duke of Savoy. Vaud was overrun, the Pays de Gex, Chablais in Geneva and a part of Faucigny were conquered. In a few weeks all the country bordering on Lake Leman was in the hands of the Swiss. It was between 1536 and 1564, after which Berne had to disgorge much of her conquests, that the Swiss Confederation attained its maximum territorial expansion.

The Catholic Cantons were perturbed by these conquests, for they perceived quite clearly that the Catholic regions which had been conquered by Berne would be subjected to forcible conversion. Geneva's alliance with Berne and Zürich gave to Geneva the practical advantages equivalent to those enjoyed by members of the Swiss Confederation, but formal admission to the Federation was withheld. The Catholic Cantons in 1572 and in 1573 refused to admit Geneva, and in 1584 imposed a similar veto on the admission of Strasbourg which was at that time under Protestant influence. The Catholic Cantons were determined to maintain the *status quo*, and not to upset the delicate and precarious balance between Catholic and Protestant Cantons by the admission of additional Protestant Cantons. There was a moment when it seemed as if relations between Catholics and Protestants might be improved, but the motive of reconciliation did no credit to either party.

The terrible peasants' war of 1653 cut right across religious differences. Catholic and Protestant Governments united in pitiless suppression of the social revolution, but the co-operation between men of the same class and different creeds was only temporary. The first and second wars of Willmergen (1656, 1712) were religious wars in the first of which the Protestants were defeated, and in the second victorious. If the Protestant Cantons had desired to exploit their victory in an effort to eliminate Catholicism from Switzerland, they would have had to reckon with foreign intervention. Switzerland has survived because religious and racial minorities have always been protected against exploitation or extermination by the fact that they enjoyed powerful support outside their frontiers.

Zwingli had started the practice of alliances, not between Switzerland as a whole, but between the Cantons united by religious faith with those of the same faith beyond their borders. The Catholic Cantons followed this example and allied themselves with Austria in 1529 and with Spain in 1557, but these alliances were defensive and more in the nature of an insurance that Austria would support the Catholic Cantons, if they were attacked by the Protestant Cantons, than alliance in the more usual sense of the term, for the Catholic Cantons accepted no obligation to take part in any war between Austria and France. On the contrary, the Swiss principle of perpetual neutrality has its roots in these alliances. Because the Protestant and Catholic Cantons had ties of sympathy with rival powers, it was impossible for Switzerland as a whole to take part in wars between rival powers without destroying the precarious unity of the Swiss Confederation. Curiously enough the Catholic Cantons did not regard their alliances with Austria and Spain as inconsistent with the alliance between France and the Swiss Confederation, an alliance which came into being shortly after Marignano (1515) and persisted right up to the invasion of Switzerland by the armies of revolutionary France. Indeed the lamentably poor resistance which the Swiss opposed to the French invaders in 1799 was partly due to the fact that they found it difficult to believe that France, their ancient protector and ally, had been transformed by the Revolution into an enemy and oppressor.

The French of the seventeenth and eighteenth centuries were as anxious to maintain a balance of power in Europe and to prevent any one power establishing an undisputed hegemony as were the British in the eighteenth, nineteenth and twentieth centuries. The independence and neutrality of Switzerland was as important to France in those centuries as was the independence of Belgium to Britain in more recent times, and because France wanted Switzerland to be strong she did her best to reconcile Cantons divided by religion in contrast to Austria whose interest lay in aggravating Swiss religious differences.

France's primary interest was to prevent Europe being dominated by Austria and Spain, great Catholic powers. France succeeded in maintaining excellent relations with both the Catholic and the Protestant Cantons, even, as we shall see in a later chapter, when the Huguenots were appealing to Calvin's Geneva for military support. Her success was mainly due to the fact that her internal policy of supporting the Catholic Church appealed to the Catholic Cantons, and her external policy of resistance to the great Catholic powers of Austria and Spain appealed no less strongly to the Protestant Cantons.

5. Swiss Neutrality

One of the more important indirect effects of the Reformation on Switzerland was, as we have seen, to impose on the Swiss the principle of perpetual neutrality.

Now Swiss neutrality has been of immense benefit not only to Switzerland but also to Europe in both world wars, and it is perhaps inevitable that the doctrine of neutrality should have acquired a quasi-religious flavour in the minds of the Swiss, as if isolationism were intrinsically and inevitably nobler than intervention. On the balance, Switzerland has gained (and Europe has gained) from Swiss neutrality, but there has been loss as well as gain, for life is a choice of sacrifices. On this point two distinguished Swiss historians, Gonzague de Reynold, a Catholic, and William Martin, a Protestant, would seem to be in substantial agreement.

" Nothing is more false," writes William Martin, " than to consider our neutrality as a Revelation. It was the result of the inability of the Swiss in the sixteenth century to co-operate. It is not an idea. It is a fact. It is not a principle, it is a negation."

" Switzerland," writes Gonzague de Reynold, " had to resign herself, little by little, to the neutrality which, though one tries to transform it into an ideal, remains an emasculation for every vital nation."

But perhaps what remains of " vital " Germany may envy the " emasculation " to which the Swiss consented when they made permanent neutrality the cornerstone of their foreign policy.

E

Chapter VI

NAPOLEONIC INTERLUDE

1. Switzerland in the Eighteenth Century

AT the end of the eighteenth century Switzerland consisted of thirteen virtually sovereign Cantons:— Uri, Schwyz, Unterwalden, Lucerne, Zug, Zürich, Glarus, Berne (together forming the eight Old Cantons), and in addition, Appenzel, Fribourg, Solothurn, Basel and Schaffhausen. This Confederation ruled over various subject territories and bailiwicks. Morat and Grandson, for instance, were held jointly by Berne and Fribourg. The Confederation was allied to independent States, which subsequently became Cantons of the Confederation. In practice there was very little difference between the relations of one Confederate Canton with another, and the relations of a Confederate Canton with the allied States, such as the Grisons, Valais, Neuchâtel, and Geneva. The links between Protestant Berne and Catholic Lucerne were no stronger than between Protestant Zürich and the independent State of the Grisons, which was mainly Protestant, for the Confederate Cantons were, in effect, autonomous States. There was no Federal Army. Each Canton had its own militia, its own customs and its own currency. The difficulties of travel were still further aggravated by the fact that the rate of exchange in some Cantons varied with the amount exchanged. In some cases Confederate Cantons waged war on each other, as did Protestant Zürich and Berne against the Five Catholic Cantons in 1712. Sometimes one group of Cantons would form a separate alliance, as, for instance, the alliance in 1715 of the Catholic Cantons with Louis XIV. But in spite of these divergent interests, a growing sense of Swiss solidarity developed through the centuries, the conviction of the imperative necessity for a defensive union, not only between the Confederate Cantons but also between the Confederation and the independent States.

The Swiss Confederation and allied States presented a bewildering mosaic of different forms of government. The pure democracy of the Landesgemeinde still survived in the old Catholic rural Cantons where laws were enacted and alliances approved by the entire adult population, but elsewhere there had been a gradual decline of democratic institutions. " Even the Reformation," writes Mrs. Lina Hug, a Swiss Protestant, " led the way to this decline by lodging all power, political, fiscal, moral and educational, in the hands of governments." Zürich was governed by a guild aristocracy. Protestant Berne and Catholic Lucerne and Fribourg by patrician aristocracies.

2. Impatient Liberators

The Revolutionary Directory in Paris was desperately in need of funds. Napoleon's victories in Italy had left them with large armies on their hands which they could neither employ, pay nor feed. The Bernese treasury was alleged to be bursting with gold. The Swiss countryside was rich and capable of supporting large armies of liberators. Clearly the sooner that Switzerland was " liberated " the better, if not for *all* concerned, at least for those who were extremely concerned by their own shortage of cash.

It was not the Bolsheviks, but the French who invented the lucrative technique of liberating countries from their oppressors. The Jacobins hated the Swiss for many reasons. The aristocratic government of Cantons such as Berne and Zürich was *ipso facto* offensive, and they had aggravated their offence by sheltering the émigrés and by their unconcealed sympathy with those reactionary enemies of the Revolution, England and Austria. When Soviet

Russia demanded that this or that British or American Diplomatist be expelled on the ground that he had been organising counter revolution they merely followed the precedent set by the French when they demanded that the Bernese should expel Mr. William Wickham, the British Minister. To avoid embarrassing his hosts Mr. Wickham left of his own accord. The French were encouraged in their plans of aggression by a fifth column of Swiss Jacobins who had founded a " Club Helvetique " in Paris during the early days of the Revolution. In the autumn of 1797 Napoleon sent for Peter Ochs of Basel, for much the same reasons that Hitler sent for Quisling in 1940. And no doubt Peter Ochs, like Quisling, was ready to do all in his power to establish " the New Order." Meanwhile French agents in Switzerland were doing what they could to foment class war, but without marked success. Many Swiss had grievances against the ruling classes and the Vaudois and other bailiwicks hated the autocratic rule of Berne but there was no widespread dynamic discontent and no evidence whatever of any desire for French " liberation." Switzerland remained calm and peaceful in spite of the underground work of the would-be liberators. Even the presence of French troops on the frontier of Vaud was not the real cause of the rising in Lausanne, and the Lausannois, who were only interested in liberating themselves from their Bernese rulers, lost the respect of the French by their failure loudly to demand French assistance. All of which was maddening for the French Generals whose impatient troops were champing on the frontier, waiting for the word which was to release them on their mission of liberation, a mission in the course of which they had every intention of liberating the Bernese treasury of superfluous gold. Finally General Menard on some trivial pretext penetrated into the territory of Vaud in order to liberate the Vaudois from the hated rule of Berne. On March 5th Berne fell, and with Berne, the old Confederation. The liberator, like the labourer, is worthy of his hire. Vaud was presented with an enormous bill for her liberation. " France is not wealthy enough," the Swiss were told, " to liberate Europe gratuitously. She is therefore entitled to indemnify herself from the liberated nations by seizing the goods of the State, the Church and the aristocracy." On entering Berne the victorious general sent twenty-four million francs in specie and securities to France, and retained a further two million for himself and his entourage. The museum and art galleries were plundered. Even the bears from the bear pit were sent to Paris. The French then proceeded to impose upon Switzerland the " Helvetic Constitution," an attempt to replace the ancient Federation of quasi-autonomous Cantons by a centralised bureaucratic, unitary state controlled by a " Directory " of five on the French model. The oldest democracies in Europe, the Catholic Cantons round the shores of Lake Lucerne, were naturally reluctant to surrender their ancient liberties to those who in the name of " Liberty, Equality and Fraternity " were preparing to impose upon Switzerland a despotism far more irksome than that of the Habsburgs against which the Forest Cantons had revolted, but their resistance was short-lived.

Lucerne was occupied without difficulty, but under the command of Alois von Reding, the hero of one of Wordsworth's poems, Schwyz offered a desperate resistance. Women dug trenches, dragged the cannon up the mountain sides and even took part in the actual fighting, but the heroic Schwyzers were forced, after some initial successes, to surrender on May 4th, 1798. The revolt in Nidwalden, which is described in Chapter XI, ended on September 9th with the historic massacre at Stans. From 1798 until the fall of Napoleon Switzerland was, in effect, a protectorate of France.

The subjugation of Switzerland profoundly shocked many who, until then, had supported the French Revolution.

Switzerland was the symbol of freedom, the country in which a primitive democracy had obtained its first victories against reactionary feudalism. The attack upon Switzerland by a Power claiming to be in the vanguard of progress produced much the same effect as the attack on democratic Finland by Soviet Russia in 1939. Wordsworth wrote the famous sonnet (*Thoughts of a Briton on the subjugation of Switzerland*) which begins:

> Two Voices are there; one is of the sea,
> One of the mountains; each a mighty voice:
> In both from age to age thou didst rejoice,
> They were thy chosen music, Liberty!

Coleridge's repudiation was even more decisive:

> Forgive me, Freedom: O forgive those dreams,
> I hear thy voice, I hear thy loud lament,
> From bleak Helvetia's icy caverns sent—
> I hear thy groans upon her blood-stained streams.
> Heros, that for your peaceful country perished,
> Any ye that, fleeing, spot your mountain snows,
> With bleeding wounds, forgive me, that I cherished
> One thought that ever blessed your cruel foes!
> To scatter rage and traitorous guilt
> Where Peace her jealous home had built;
> A patriot race to disinherit
> Of all that made their stormy wilds so dear;
> And with inexpiable spirit
> To taint the bloodless freedom of the mountaineer.
> O France, that mockest Heaven, adulterous, blind,
> And patriot only in pernicious toils!
> Are these thy boasts, Champion of human kind?
> To mix with Kings in the low lust of sway,
> Yell in the hunt, and share the murderous prey,
> To insult the shrine of Liberty with spoils
> From freemen torn, to tempt and to betray?

History seldom repeats herself exactly. France, our enemy when she invaded Switzerland, did not subsequently become our ally, and consequently those who were shocked

by the invasion of Switzerland never felt under any obligation to prove that the Revolutionary Armies had only
invaded Switzerland to anticipate an Austrian invasion of
France.

3. Stratford Canning in Switzerland

Napoleon's fiasco in Russia and his defeat at Leipzig,
October 18th, 1813, made it expedient for him to reduce
his commitments, with the result that Switzerland, which
had been for years in a condition of latent revolt against
the French occupation, regained her independence without
having to fight for it.   In the summer of 1814 Lord Castlereagh sent the most brilliant of the younger British Diplo-
matists to Zürich which was then the capital of the Swiss
Confederation.

Three Cannings are commemorated by statues in West-
minster Abbey: George Canning, the great statesman, his
son Charles, Earl Canning, first Viceroy of India, and his
cousin, Stratford Canning, Viscount Stratford de Recliffe,
the first Ambassador to be thus honoured and perhaps the
greatest Ambassador in our history.   Tennyson's tribute
to " the voice of England in the East " was not poetic licence.
For a long period Stratford Canning* exercised a dominant
influence in Constantinople.

Stratford Canning fell in love with Switzerland the first
moment of his arrival.   From Zürich on July 5th, 1814, he
writes:

> Put on your spurs, mount your yacht, and come the
> shortest possible way to this delicious country.   When
> once here, you will acknowledge that you have spent
> twenty years of your life most unprofitably.   In short
> you are, and must be, an owl till you set foot in this
> land of liberty and cocked hats.   The finest mountains—

* It is curious to note that two men, both of whom in their different
ways were destined to have great influence on Switzerland, Stratford
Canning and Byron, should have played on opposite sides in the first
Eton and Harrow match at Lord's.

the greenest hills—the richest plains—the neatest houses—the best inns—the most limpid streams, and for aught I know the most delightful fair ones, ever yet beheld in this transitory sphere! Elysium and Mahomet's seventh heaven are mere jokes to this earthly anticipation of Paradise!! You will be particularly happy too to know, for my sake, that ceremony is a plant unknown to these simple regions. I am established at the Hotel de l'Epée in a single room, which serves me " for parlour and kitchen and all," surrounded by Deputies and illustrious travellers, who turn out of the neighbouring rooms, in swords and cocked hats, to pay me *leurs devoirs*. About five minutes afterwards I go out of my room, take a turn in the passage hat in hand, and return the visit as if I had just arrived from the other side of the mountains.

Stratford Canning was a realist as far as contemporary Switzerland was concerned but an uncritical romanticist about Swiss origins. His enthusiasm for William Tell evoked from his Austrian colleague, Baron Schraut, the indignant reply that his " favourite Tell was an assassin." Knowing nothing of the social structure or long military experience of those who won the battle of Morgarten he accepted the traditional conception of " the simple half-awed peasant opposed to the feudal horseman in his glittering panoply."

The allied representatives in Switzerland were charged with the task of attempting to obtain Swiss agreement for a new constitution. The Swiss Cantons had reacted against Napoleonic centralisation by an enthusiastic return to their old particularism. The Cantons had their own currencies, their own measures of weight, their own tariffs, valid against all other Cantons, and even their own armies. A weak and disunited Switzerland would, so the allies felt, be in danger of falling once again under French influence. The allied representatives in Switzerland were therefore primarily concerned to secure the adoption of a

constitution which would provide a sound basis for an independent, united and neutral Switzerland. Their success
was only partial. None the less Stratford Canning was to
make a notable contribution to Swiss unity before his
mission ended.

His first impressions were, as we have seen, very
favourable:

> The people are exceedingly good. Not the more
> poetical for being in the midst of rocks and waterfalls,
> and rather given to matter of fact and prosing but with
> a goodness of heart, and in general a straightforwardness
> which would reconcile one to more determined faults
> than those. What you have heard of their simplicity is
> true. Luxury is almost unknown. People who rise
> and sleep with the sun, and dine soon after midday,
> cannot be very dissipated.

> After all this I need not tell you that I am perfectly
> contented with my republican situation, although
> some feelings of regret may have been excited by
> not having had a single opportunity of wearing my
> Windsor uniform. The Sovereign of the Confederacy
> returned my first visit on foot, with a cocked-hat and
> sword for his only regalia and their Deputies have such
> an aversion to finery that they make their servants wear
> their distinctive robe of ceremony, while they themselves
> proceed to the Diet in suits of indiscriminate black. . . .

> The people in this country are prodigious prosers, and
> there are something between twenty and thirty deputa-
> tions from different parts of Switzerland successively
> coming to me with long stories about justice, rights,
> expediency, and necessity. The next drain upon time
> is the unconscionable hour of dinner. If I am not to
> dine at two (not two in the morning, but two after noon),
> not a soul would come near me; and it is necessary for
> the progress of business that the Deputies should be
> duly fed.

On October 23rd, 1814, Castlereagh summoned him to
Vienna. The Swiss deputies to the Congress paid him

visits which had not, so he complains, " the angelic quality of being ' few and far between ' . . ."

There was also the class of " mediatised " claimants who looked to Congress for their reinstatement, and passed their time in recommending their pretensions to everyone who was supposed to have the slightest influence. The Abbot of St. Gall was one of the dispossessed princes, and I cannot easily forget a dinner at which I enjoyed the questionable privilege of sitting next to him at table. He knew no modern language but his own, and that was a sealed vessel to me. All that we had in common was Latin, which I was not in the habit of talking, and which he pronounced with an accent entirely foreign to my ears. The dinner lasted three mortal hours, and the Abbot thought it an excellent opportunity for putting me in full possession of his grievances, his rights and his hopes.

After Napoleon's return from Elba it was Stratford Canning's duty to persuade the Swiss to take an auxiliary part in the grand coalition against Napoleon. " None were desirous of incurring the expenses of war, and provoking the ill-will of their vindictive neighbours. They felt the necessity of arming, but thought in general that they could not begin too soon to be neutral."

If you ask an educated Swiss how many times the Swiss have fought on foreign soil during five centuries he will, of course, cite the Swiss campaign in North Italy which ended with the defeat of Marignano (1515), and he may, or may not, remember the Bernese conquest of North Savoy in 1536, but he will almost certainly forget a rather inglorious episode, the Swiss invasion of French territory *after* Waterloo. Some French communities on the borders of Switzerland asked for Swiss occupation to save them from being occupied by their Austrian enemies. The chiefs of the Swiss Army, against the wishes of the Government, invaded France on July 3rd and took part under the command of Archduke John of Austria in the siege of Huningue. Five days later, the regiments of Aargau, St. Gall and the Ticine, who like the Swiss deputies at Vienna, "thought in general that they could not begin too soon to be neutral" mutinied. "We had no reason," writes William Martin, "to be proud of this campaign, which was initiated by the insubordination of the Commanders at a moment when there was no longer any risk in being courageous and which was ended by the mutiny of the soldiers. But it was our last campaign on foreign soil and we cannot therefore suppress it from our history. It is surprising to note how completely it has vanished from the memory of the Swiss people."

Stratford Canning left Zürich for Berne at the end of 1815. His comments on the view from Berne remind me of the English traveller who remarked that Holland was more beautiful than Switzerland seeing that "there are no mountains to intercept the view." "The country around is agreeable," writes Stratford Canning, "and if not overstocked with woods of dismal fir and blocked up along one whole side by enormous mountains of snow would be sufficiently like England to delight an English eye."

After prolonged negotiations the Swiss were eventually persuaded to accept the "Federal Compact." The Federal Compact, like the treaty of Vienna, was the work of statesmen not of doctrinaires. In a letter to a friend, Stratford Canning defined their guiding principle, a principle which was too often ignored by the victors in both world wars:

Every day I feel more and more convinced that it is much better to leave a nation its customs and habits and to a certain degree its prejudices than to impose upon it the more finished system if that system be inconsistent with what it has been accustomed to love and venerate for ages. I have no faith in constitutions that look pretty on paper, those which have been most durable and have best answered their end have grown gradually with circumstances, and are rather a series of precedents reduced into rules and laws, not a system composed to anticipate events.

The architects of the Treaty of Vienna and the subsidiary pacts were lucky not to be subject to demagogic pressure. The peace between Great Britain and France which was implemented at Vienna has endured to this day. Stratford Canning did not achieve all that he hoped for but it was partly due to his efforts that the reorganisation of Switzerland was completed on September 12th, 1814, by the admission to the Confederation of the former " Allied States " of Geneva, Neuchâtel and the Valais. In 1816 Canning drew up a memorial in which he advocated the creation of a Federal military school and a standing military authority. " These reforms," writes the distinguished Swiss historian, the late Professor Wilhelm Oeschli of the University of Zürich, " were not new, but only such as the superior officers of Switzerland had long demanded as indispensable. But the Memorial of the esteemed representative of Great Britain has this advantage that it stiffened the back of the supporters of military reform. So far Stratford Canning is not wrong when he claims for England the honour of having given the impulse to the Federal army reform of 1817, to which our military organisation in the nineteenth century goes back."

Chapter VII

A VERY CIVIL WAR

THE period from 1815 to 1848 was a period of growing tension between the champions of Cantonal rights and the Centralists. The former took their stand on the letter of the law. The Federal Pact was a treaty guaranteed by the Powers and accepted by the Cantons, a treaty which could not be revised except by a unanimous vote of the Cantons. In this they were supported by the Powers who regarded the Pact as their work, and as an integral element in the *droit publique européen*. The Catholic Cantons dreaded any increase of the powers of the central Government, in which Catholics would inevitably be in the minority.

Those who maintained that the Pact could not be changed without a unanimous decision of the Cantons were on impregnable ground from a legal point of view, but their position was untenable, for the whole tendency of the age was against them. It was absurd to suppose that Europe (or the Swiss) could tolerate indefinitely 25 sovereign, or virtually sovereign, states within the frontiers of Switzerland, or that Swiss industry could compete with the outside world so long as this small country was divided by customs barriers. There were, to take only one example, no less than 50 different measures of weight in Switzerland.

The differences between the two parties would in time have reached a peaceable settlement had not *odium theologicum* been imported into what was otherwise a political controversy. Unfortunately, on January 20th, 1834, seven Cantons, six of whom were Protestant, and one of whom was under the temporary rule of an anti-clerical Radical majority, met at Baden and agreed on a programme of ecclesiastical reform which was bound to cause great offence to the Catholics, for it included, among other proposals, a demand that no Bishop should be appointed without Government sanction, and that Seminaries should be subject to state control.

The Baden proposals were formally condemned by the ecclesiastical authorities, and on January 9th, 1841, a clerical revolt at Villmergen gave the Radicals of Aargau a pretext for the closing of all the eight convents in the Canton. This action was a violation of the Federal Pact which expressly guaranteed the existence of the convents. The indignation of the Catholics led to the immediate overthrow of the Radical Government in control of Lucerne (one of the seven Cantons which met at Baden) and to the placing in power of men who were to become in due course the leaders of the Sonderbund.

The Diet having passed a law to suppress the Jesuits, the Government of Lucerne promptly invited the Jesuits to take control of the principal schools and colleges in Lucerne. On December 8th, 1844, and again on March 31st, 1845, armed bands formed on the territory of Aargau and Berne with the approval of the Governments of these Cantons, and with arms provided from their arsenals, raided the territory of Lucerne. One of the Catholic leaders was assassinated in mysterious circumstances.

It was not surprising that the Catholics should have secretly concluded on December 11th, 1845, a defensive alliance (the Sonderbund) between the Catholic Cantons of Lucerne, Uri, Schwyz, Unterwalden, Zug, Fribourg and the Valais. Two years later, on November 4th, 1847, the Diet declared war on the Sonderbund.

Austria and France sympathised with the Sonderbund as the embodiment of conservative principles. Metternich

was anxious to intervene. " The British Cabinet," writes
Oeschli, " was the only one which exhibited a sympathetic
understanding of the aims of Liberal Switzerland. . . .
On principle he (Lord Palmerston) was opposed to any
intervention in Switzerland. By apparently acceding to
the desires of the other Cabinets he most adroitly secured
for himself the leadership of the anti-Swiss movement,
being thus enabled to blunt its point and to delay it until
it was too late. . . . Switzerland, by her steadfast
resistance to the Sonderbund, won definite freedom from
the yoke of the foreigner. The service which in this matter
free England had rendered her cannot and never will be
forgotten."

The war was in every respect a very civil war. Only
71 soldiers were killed on the Federal side, and rather less
on the side of the Sonderbund. General Dufour, the
Protestant Commander of the Federal forces, was a man of
high principles, determined that the civil war should leave
as small a legacy of bitterness as possible. Here is a passage
from his proclamation to the Federal forces:—

> Disarm prisoners, but do not insult or injure them.
> On the contrary, treat them as kindly as possible. Allow
> them to return to their homes if they give their word of
> honour not to take arms again. At all costs prevent
> violation of religious establishments. Carry your respect
> for these places to the point of not billeting troops in
> them, and place guards to protect them.

Dufour's proclamation was characteristically Swiss in its
determination to push nothing to extremes. It is this
instinct for compromise which alone has enabled Switzerland to survive. There was no aftermath of the Swiss
Civil War to compare with the tragic period of so-called
" Reconstruction " after the American Civil War.

The Swiss Civil War began on November 4th and ended
on November 30th, 1847. The fact that hostilities lasted
for so short a time, and that the casualties were so few,

strengthened the forces making for moderation. Victors and vanquished collaborated in the preparation of the new Federal Constitution which became effective on September 12th, 1848.

The foundation of modern Switzerland dates from the acceptance of the 1848 Constitution which, with a few unimportant modifications, is still in force to-day.

Chapter VIII

WHY DEMOCRACY WORKS IN SWITZERLAND

1. Imperilled Democracy

IT is chastening to recall the complacent optimism with which President Wilson surveyed the world which American intervention had made " safe for democracy." In the nineteen-twenties it was still possible to believe that the virtues of democracy were so self-evident that a world which had been liberated from Kaisers, Tsars and Kings would never again return to such reactionary régimes. And within a few short years a world saved *from* democracy was, in effect, the ambition both of right-wing and left-wing revolutionaries.

England only became a democracy in this century. In the nineteenth century it was still an oligarchy, for the essential difference between oligarchy (the rule of the few) and democracy (the rule of the people) is that in the former the franchise is restricted and in the latter unrestricted. Until the turn of the century the franchise was always dependent on some slight property qualification. To-day the majority of mankind are governed, not by democratic, but by authoritarian régimes. Is this to be the pattern of the future? Was Aristotle right when he declared that democracy is an ephemeral and transitional form of government, half way between oligarchy and tyranny? Are his modern disciples justified in their assertion that representative government is only secure if the franchise is limited to citizens with some property, and that adult-suffrage democracy inevitably leads to the plundering of the thrifty and capable minority by the feckless majority until bankruptcy forces the establishment of an autocracy? Certainly Aristotle's thesis can be illustrated by the history of one South American republic after another, republics in which the transference of power from an oligarchical minority to a democratic majority resulted in financial chaos. On the other hand, the most stable Government in the history of Christendom was the oligarchical Republic of Venice.

Those who distrust democracy and who despair of a restoration of oligarchy, in however mild a form, should study the constitution and history of Switzerland. Here at least is one country in which democracy works, one country in which democracy seems to possess reserves which enable it to resist the kind of pressure which has proved fatal to other democracies. Even in the dark days when Switzerland was entirely surrounded by the Axis and when Russia was collaborating with Germany, and America neutral, Swiss Quislings failed to collect any effective following. Later, when Soviet Russia was at the peak of her popularity and prestige, Swiss Communists were equally unsuccessful. Before attempting to explain the stability and effectiveness of Swiss democracy, it will be best to begin by a brief description of the manner in which Switzerland is governed.

2. The Swiss Constitution

The constitution of 1848, though it transformed Switzerland from a loose federation of twenty-five virtually sovereign states into a Federal Republic, still left great powers to the Cantons. A Swiss Gemeinde is a collection of individuals and families who live in a particular district. A Gemeinde is a miniature Canton, and has been described as " one of the cells of which the social body is composed." Some of the Gemeinde are rich, others are poor, but all alike have a large measure of self-government and are empowered to levy taxes for local services, such as the local police (there are also, of course, the Cantonal police), the local fire brigade, and so forth. The Gemeinde superintends the schools and looks after its own poor.

If the Gemeinde is one of the cells, the Canton is one of the limbs of which the social body is composed. Every Swiss citizen is subject to a double sovereignty. There is the Federal sovereignty and the Cantonal sovereignty.

The Cantons are really sovereign states which have surrendered to the Federal Government certain sovereign powers. The Swiss citizen pays his taxes not to the Federal Government but, in the first instance, to his Gemeinde, and in the second instance to his Canton. The Federal Government alone can declare war, make peace, and conclude alliances. The Federal Government controls the army, collects duty on imports, and has the exclusive right to coin money and to issue banknotes. On the strength of emergency legislation, dating from the first world war, the Federal Government has the right to levy certain direct taxes, such as the National Defence Tax. Efforts are being made in a Federal finance reform Act to put the question of Federal taxation on a constitutional basis. Each Canton still retains a large measure of sovereignty and its own Parliament. It was only on January 1st, 1942, that the Cantons ceased to have their own separate criminal law and civil code. Since January 1st, 1942, the Federal Civil Code is valid in all Cantons.

The Federal Tribunal at Lausanne decides disputes between the Federation and the Cantons themselves, and between corporations and individuals on the one side and the Confederation on the other side. The Federal Tribunal is also the final court of appeal for all civil actions where the point at dispute involves a larger sum than 4,000 francs.

The two political powers whereby Federal sovereignty is exercised are the Federal Assembly (Bundesversammlung) and the Federal Council (Bundesrat).

The Federal Assembly is composed of two Chambers, the National Council (Nationalrat) and the Council of the States (Ständerat). When these two Chambers meet in joint sessions they form the Federal Assembly.

The Federal Assembly, being therefore composed of representatives of the people and of representatives of the Cantons, symbolises the double sovereignty which exists in Switzerland.

The National Council consists of 194 members, and is elected by ballot every four years, there being one deputy for every 22,000 inhabitants.

The Council of the States is composed of forty-four deputies. Each Canton returns two deputies, and the method of electing these deputies is left to the Cantons. In some Cantons the deputies are chosen by the legislative bodies, in others by the people, either in Landesgemeinde or by ballot.

The Nationalrat and Ständerat practically only sit in joint session for the election of the members of the Bundesrat (the Cabinet) and for the election of the judges of the Federal court at Lausanne. Both Chambers are of the same political importance.

All Federal laws, after being passed by both Chambers, must be submitted to a referendum of the people if thirty thousand vote-possessing citizens, or eight Cantons, demand this referendum. The people also possess the right to initiate legislation involving changes in the Federal Constitution.

Whereas the Referendum is beneficial, for it acts as a conservative check on ill-digested legislation, the Initiative is less advantageous, for it enables fifty thousand cranks to throw the country into a turmoil over a Bill which has no chance of passing. The Capital Levy proposals, for instance, which involved the insertion of a new article into the Constitution, were voted on as the result of a Socialistic Initiative. Foreigners who did not appreciate the distinction between a Referendum and an Initiative were much alarmed. The inevitable and overwhelming rejection of the Capital Levy was foreseen by all competent observers.

The Federal Council, or Bundesrat, is the executive Government of the Confederation, and is composed of seven members elected by the Federal Assembly. The Bundesrat, in other words, is the Swiss Cabinet, but, unlike our own Cabinet, it is not composed entirely of members of the same party.

Switzerland has enjoyed the advantages, or disadvantages, of a coalition Government for the last sixty years. A Government is none the less a coalition even if one party is not represented, but the Swiss Government became a coalition of all the parties that have ever counted for anything after the inclusion of a Catholic in the nineties and of a Socialist, an old Grindelwald friend of mine, Herr Bundesdrat Nobs, in 1943.

To-day the Bundesrat, which can best be translated as the Federal Council, includes recruits from all the principal political parties (including the Socialists) and representatives of the main religious and racial minorities. It is an accepted practice that every Federal Councillor is automatically re-elected, and that the different Councillors take it in turn to become President of the Confederation and Chairman of the Federal Council in rotation, the term of office for the President being strictly limited to one year. There could be no better guarantee against extremism than the partnership in government between Federal Councillors recruited from different political parties. The Socialist inevitably gravitates to the left centre and the Conservative to the right centre, and a workable compromise is thereby achieved.

In the discussion following a lecture at the Alpine Club Mr. Leo Amery, at one time Secretary of State for India, pointed out that the British system of party government had worked reasonably well in our country because of our national genius for compromise, but he added that it had been disastrous for most countries which had adopted it, and that he had for many years advocated for India a constitution based rather on Swiss than on British precedents.

3.   The Modest Rôle of Swiss Politicians

A friend of mine who was catching an early train from Berne once found himself sitting next to the President of the Swiss Federation in a tram carrying the President to his office which opened at 7.15 a.m. (like every other Government office).   If any other Swiss in the tram had recognised him it would have been regarded as very bad form to have made the President conscious of the fact.   You never find in a Swiss paper personal paragraphs about the Federal Councillors.   The wives of Federal Councillors or of deputies are never asked to open bazaars or to subscribe to local charities.   Once a year the Federal Council invites the Diplomatic Corps to dinner.   During the rest of the year the entertaining of the Diplomatic Corps is left to the old patrician families of Berne.

The Federal Council can neither make laws, nor veto laws which have been enacted in accordance with the constitution, but so far as administration is concerned they are an oligarchy with great powers.   Each Federal Councillor is a king in his own department.   The Swiss constitution provides no means for resolving an irreconcilable clash between the Federal Council and the Federal Assembly and no method of dissolving or dismissing a Federal Council which has been obnoxious to the Federal Assembly until the term of office has been completed. Federal Councillors are, in effect, elected for life, for though they must submit themselves for re-election every four years only one Federal Councillor since 1848 has offered himself for, and failed to secure, re-election.   Translate this into English terms. Can you conceive any other democracy having such confidence in the wisdom of their rulers that they provided no means of getting rid of a Cabinet, and assumed that Cabinet Ministers once appointed would continue to be re-elected? I was in Switzerland when Mr. Churchill's Government was defeated in the General Election of 1945, and happened to meet a Swiss Socialist. He was as shocked and horrified as the rest of the country. That Mr. Churchill should cease to be a Minister of the Crown after his pre-eminent services was something he just could not begin to understand.

If " prestige " be measured by publicity and fame (or notoriety), our Cabinet Ministers enjoy far more prestige than the Federal Councillors, but they do not command more respect. There is no Parliamentary office in Great Britain from Cabinet Minister to member of Parliament which commands the respect that it did a hundred years ago. The status of a Cabinet Minister, so far as public esteem is concerned, depends to-day far less on membership of the Cabinet than on his personal achievements when in office. There are countries where the mere fact of being a politician creates a prejudice in the minds of decent people, for in those countries politicians usually retire with a fortune from the political arena.

Now the complete probity of Federal Councillors is accepted as axiomatic in Switzerland. Most of them are men who could earn ten times as much in industry. Their modest way of life and their shrinking from publicity stamps them as men who have gone into politics, not for what they can get out of it, but for what they can put into it. The Swiss may be uninterested in Federal Councillors as personalities for they attract no crowds, and are treated by their fellow citizens with a kind of republican simplicity, but they enjoy an immense respect. And because they represent the nation, rather than the party to which they belong, and are chosen to administer the affairs of the nation, the Swiss would find it difficult to admit that they were no longer worthy of their confidence. In re-electing a Federal Councillor the Swiss are, in effect, passing a vote of confidence in their own political sagacity.

Members of Parliament will criticise the administration on points of detail but in the final analysis they will support its authority. Of course the Government is criticised, particularly by the press in French Switzerland or by the Socialists, but both Houses of Parliament, Nationalrat and Ständerat, will in the final analysis support the authority of the Federal Council. Particularly the Ständerat; and this is all the stranger because the Ständerat in which each Canton is represented by two members was intended by the framers of the 1848 constitution to act as a check on centralisation, but the members of the Ständerat, being more often than not Cantonal magistrates, have a natural understanding of, and sympathy with, the difficulties of power and an instinctive tendency to support the central Government, though in theory at least, elected to keep a watchful eye on " ces messieurs de Berne."

The Swiss word for parochialism is " kantönligeist," literally " the spirit of the little canton." Kantönligeist is much the same as the spirit which inspires the champions of State rights in America against the Federal Government. Of course " kantönligeist " is very irritating to planners in general and to Socialists in particular, but congenial to those reactionary folk who are opposed to the concentration of power in the hands of the few.

The two world wars have made things easy for the centralisers, but the kantönligeist is still vigorous in Switzerland, and indeed has become more militant since the war. One of the greatest assets of Switzerland is the *disunity* of the country. Whereas in England resistance to the encroaching tyranny of bureaucracy can be represented or misrepresented as the resistance of diehard Tories to modern progress, in Switzerland this resistance to centralisation is associated not so much with political as with linguistic and racial parties.   Geneva, for instance, tends to be critical of the Federal Government because Geneva is *ipso facto* critical of anything which is located in Berne.   The *disunity* of Switzerland is the best guarantee of Swiss freedom.

4.   *Kantönligeist*

Whether or not centralisation increases efficiency is a question of opinion, but it would be difficult for the most ardent of centralisers to deny that centralisation is the enemy of culture.   Culture cannot be mass produced by a central organisation.   Every great culture has its roots in regionalism, that is in regional traditions and regional loyalties.   There are continents which have a narrower range of cultures than little Switzerland.   Zürich, for instance, is a great industrial centre, modern and progressive, secular in its ethos in spite of a large Catholic immigration.   Its Summer School gives a warm welcome to advanced Socialists such as my friend Mr. Kingsley Martin and Mr. Richard Crossman.   The town of Zürich is at one end of a lake, the other end of which belongs to Schwyz, the oldest, and still the most conservative, of the Catholic Cantons.   The citizens of Zürich, this Athens by the Limmat, are as anxious as were the Athenians, to whom St. Paul preached, " to tell or to hear of any new thing," but a fast car will carry you in little more than an hour into the heart of the Catholic Cantons of Central Switzerland, into the Maderanertal, for instance, where visitors are earnestly begged to wear stockings with their shorts, as I discovered in the course of a visit described in the last chapter of this book.   The " Kantönligeist " is only one of many forms in which the Swiss bias in favour of distribution as against centralisation finds expression.   The Swiss have been remarkably successful in preventing the concentration of landed property in the hands of the few.

The founders of Switzerland established, as we have seen (page 38), the principle of peasant proprietorship.

To-day modern legislation has reinforced the instinctive bias of the Swiss against anything which tended to concentrate the landed property in the hands of the few. " It has always been very difficult," a Swiss friend of mine explained, " to persuade a peasant to sell. He says, ' Land is worth more than money '." What infinite wisdom is crystallised in that saying.

Just before the outbreak of the second world war a rich Swiss manufacturer tried to buy part of a cow alp for he felt that if he owned the alp he would at least be sure of butter and cheese, but the Government stepped in and forbade the sale, on the ground that he was not a farmer and would have to hire somebody to run the alp for him. Ruskin would have been delighted, for the tendency of such legislation is in accordance with the Ruskinian principle—" property to whom proper."

A case in point was the reaction of the mountain people to the attempt of a brilliant businessman in Berne to start chain stores for the sale of skis, toboggans, ice axes, etc. The mountain people felt that it was far better that natives and foreigners should pay ten per cent more for their sports equipment to a free man who owned his shop and who had his roots in the village than ten per cent less to the employees of an absentee owner in Berne.

Unfortunately, the growth and development of co-operatives is tending to put the small man who owns his shop out of business.

The same ingenious businessman in Berne had another brain wave. Why not put a shop on wheels and send round a lorry full of cheap things to sell? In Zürich this innovation was welcomed. All the more so when it was gravely explained that the resistance to this innovation came from wicked capitalists who wanted to charge the poor far more than they should. At the frontier of one

Conservative agricultural Canton the lorry was overturned and wrecked, at another Canton frontier the driver of the shop on wheels was told that he would have to wait.   The necessary legislation to forbid him to enter would be passed in the course of the next twenty-four hours and meanwhile he had better spend the night in the village on the other side of the Cantonal frontier.

5. Swiss Prosperity

Swiss prosperity is not due to the war.   Of course the Swiss benefited from the fact that they were not devastated, and that they were in a position to take full advantage of the sellers' market when the war stopped, but on the balance they certainly did not make a profit from the war. The Alpine *reduit* was extremely expensive to erect, and in 1951 the Swiss were spending on their defences more than a hundred francs per head of the population (*circa* £8 per head), more than the United Kingdom was spending per head under the imminent threat of the third world war.

From 1940 to 1948 the Swiss spent per head of the population 265 francs on war charities, Red Cross, refugee collections, etc.   And this takes no account whatever of millions of francs spent by private people entertaining refugees. Swiss with very modest incomes, like my friend Herr Stäger of Mürren, who gives ski lessons, acted as host after the war for some weeks to under-nourished English children.

Anybody who suggests that the Swiss made a profit out of the war has got to prove that the extra war profits of their export trade balanced not only the loss on their hotels, but also the immense sums spent on their military budget and their charities.   I do not envy the critic who tries to defend this brief.

Swiss prosperity is mainly due to the fact that they believe in the dignity of work, and that their democracy still finds a place for duty as well as for rights. They have not ceased to revere those " Gods of the Copybook Headings " of whom Kipling wrote in his memorable prediction of 1919:—

> And after all this is accomplished, and the brave new
>   world begins,
> When all men are paid for existing and no man must pay
>   for his sins,
> As surely as Water will wet us, as surely as Fire will burn,
> The Gods of the Copybook Headings with terror and
>   slaughter return.

Dr. André Siegfried in his interesting book, *Switzerland : A Democratic Way of Life*, points out that the absence of coal and oil have " saved Switzerland from the temptations of mass production and condemned the Swiss to superiority." A double tradition, artisan, born in the uplands of the ingenuity of the peasants, and scientific, which developed from " the splendid civilisation of Switzerland's towns since the Middle Ages," have formed the basis on which Swiss qualities of industry and intelligence, coupled with advanced technique, have developed. The " technical superiority of the Swiss has a cultural basis. Even the largest Swiss industries have never lost the human touch." The Swiss still compete against the Americans because of the " patience, care and concentrated attention " of their workmen. The finish and delicacy of the finest Swiss products are unique. In the old days the Swiss exported the finest soldiers in Europe. To-day they export technicians. Colombia orders a generating station from Baden or Winterthur. Highly skilled experts accompany the machinery and unpack and assemble it and do not leave until it is put into running order. Such technical experts often stay behind as mechanics, experts and teachers. The Swiss, thus, export not only machinery, but also " the know how," and are " developing a technical diplomacy which is covering the whole world with a close network of industrial representation. Swiss emigration has become, like Swiss exports, an emigration of quality."

The principal causes of Swiss prosperity are twofold—first the high quality of their goods, and secondly hard work. Government and private enterprises work on the average forty-four to forty-eight hours per week. There is no five-day week in Switzerland.

The tourist industry is less important and less esteemed than most tourists believe. The Swiss passion for independence is still very much alive, and militates against the political ambitions of those who are connected with the tourist industry. It is very difficult for an hotelier to be elected to the Nationalrat. At the present moment I do not think that the Swiss hoteliers are represented at all. Again, the difficulties of the hotels are largely due to the support given to the peasants, and consequently to the high prices of meat, etc. A Swiss professionally interested in increasing the number of English tourists said to me: " Of course I would like the price of meat to be lowered, but the Government are none the less right to protect the peasant and to do all in their power to prevent the flight of the peasants to the towns. The religious and cultural stability of this country depends in the final analysis on the peasants. They are still by far the soundest part of our population."

Dr. Siegfried does well to draw attention to the fact that the Swiss people have been spared not only wars but revolutions. " They felt the repercussions of the revolutions of 1789 and 1848, but their roots were never severed as ours were in what was almost a surgical operation, thus preventing us from going back freely to the distant limits of our national past. No such break ever occurred in Switzerland, which enjoys direct contact with her past right back into the Middle Ages—a contact which nourishes a still living tradition." Eugene Bagger in his admirable book, *For the Heathen are Wrong*, makes, as we shall see, much the same point.

Chapter IX

THE LIFE OF AN ALPINE VALLEY

1. The Alps

WHO owns the cattle alps? Who employs the *Senns*, as the communal herdsmen are called? To whom do the cattle belong? These are questions which every intelligent mountaineer or mountain-hiker will inevitably ask, and though customs vary from valley to valley, it may be helpful to provide a general answer which is, in its main outlines, true of all Alpine valleys.

"Kührechte," the rights to graze a stipulated number of cows on the various "alps" which are the property of different Gemeinde, may either be acquired, as in some valleys, by the purchase of a piece of property which carries with it corresponding grazing rights, or may be restricted to the members of the Burgerschaft.

The Senns are employed by the Gemeinde. It is their duty to look after the cows and to transform their milk into cheese. Twice or three times in the course of the summer the owners of the cows must attend at the alps for a formal test of their cows' milk-producing capacity. On those occasions the cows are milked and the amount of milk which each cow produces is officially recorded, and this amount determines the owner's share of the communal cheeses which are distributed at the end of summer. If your cow is not feeling quite herself on these important occasions, well, it's just too bad.

"Our cattle alps," a Swiss Socialist once remarked to me, "are an excellent example of primitive socialism."

I disagreed. A communal cow alp is an example of primitive capitalism. Neither the cows nor the cheeses belong to the community. The alp is a kind of limited company of which the Senns are the Directors. The owner of cow-rights invests his cows, and draws interest in the form of cheese.

There is little danger of Switzerland evolving into a tyrant state, for individual liberty in Switzerland is based on foundations more solid than the political rhetoric of demagogues. It would puzzle most Swiss to explain why totalitarian propaganda, whether of the right or of the left, has been such a failure in Switzerland, for the conditions which render Switzerland secure against tyranny have their roots in the remote past. " In the old days," Aldous Huxley said to me in 1941, " there was always somebody to appeal to—the Emperor against the Pope, or the nobles against the King—but we are now moving towards the Moloch of the centralised totalitarian state against whose verdict there is no appeal." Switzerland, on the other hand, still maintains the saving principle of the distribution of power. The Cantons jealously preserve their rights and resist Federal centralisation. The peasantry are not subordinated to the towns, for no Swiss government would dare to ignore the claims of the peasantry. On the other hand, the urban workers have been as successful as any trade unionists in Europe in ameliorating their condition. Switzerland thus maintains a well-balanced economy between town and country, and a balance of powers as between the Cantons and the Federal Government.

Secondly, the Swiss have always believed in the distribution of property, particularly property as a means of production, such as land or a small business. The foundations of the Swiss way of life were laid in 1294, when, as we have seen, the assembled people of Schwyz resolved in public assembly that it should in future be forbidden to sell land either to ecclesiastical corporations or to strangers beyond the borders of the Canton. A Swiss member of Parliament (Nationalrat) told me that a wealthy foreigner had been trying to buy up such plots of land as were for sale in a mountain village. The reaction of the community was instinctive and final. The word went round that nobody was to sell. On the other hand, had the refugee merely wished to buy enough ground on which to build a house, with a garden attached, no obstacles would have been placed in his way.

Swiss democracy works because it is both conservative and progressive, the Tory democracy of which Disraeli dreamed, but which he never achieved. " In those fifteen months," writes Mr. Eugene Bagger in his book, *For the Heathen are Wrong*, " I came to regard Switzerland as the finest democracy in the world, a democracy based on the effort of hard thinking, and the dignity of hard work and the beauty of self-imposed discipline. It was the one democracy in Europe that was on the one hand truly democratic, and on the other hand *worked:* and this was because of all the European democracies it remained most faithful to the Christian origin of our civilisation. It was the most advanced of the European nations, because it was the most conservative."

2. Village Oligarchies

Every Swiss citizen has the right to vote for, and to offer himself for, election to the Gemeinderat of the Gemeinde in which he is domiciled. And it is to the Gemeinde that he pays his taxes. The Gemeinde controls most of the local activities, but in many Gemeinde the grazing rights, and the right to a certain amount of forest wood, still belong to an oligarchy composed of the descendants of the original Burgers. In other Gemeinde there is no distinction between the Burgers and the Einwohner— that is the Swiss citizens who are domiciled in the Gemeinde.

In some Gemeinde, as we have seen, the Kührechte (the rights to graze so many cows on the communal alps) are restricted to members of the Burgerschaft. In other Gemeinde these rights are attached to a particular property and change hands when the property is sold.

In some valleys the Burgerschaft is a completely closed oligarchy, like a House of Lords with no possibility of creating new peers. In some Cantons the Canton reserves the right to insist that a particular Burgerschaft admit a new Burger on payment of a sum to be determined by the Cantonal Government.

The classic case is the controversy between Alexander Seiler, the creator of Zermatt as a tourist centre, and the Zermatt Burgerschaft. The story of this controversy is described in Dr. Kämpfer's treatise, *Ein Burgerrechtsstreit im Wallis*.

Alexander Seiler, who built the first hotel in Zermatt, the Monte Rosa, in the early fifties, applied for membership of the Burgerschaft in June, 1871. His application was rejected, but the Valais Government supported him, and drew the attention of the Zermatt Burgerschaft to Article 10 of the Constitution, according to which any Valaisan (*not* any Swiss) who has been five years domiciled in a Gemeinde, must be granted membership of the Burgerschaft on payment of a sum to be fixed by the Cantonal Government. The Zermatt Burgerschaft appealed in succession to the Bundesrat (the Cabinet), to the Bundesversammlung (both Houses of Parliament), and finally to the Federal Court at Lausanne. Every appeal failed, but still the unconquerable oligarchy of Zermatt resisted, and it was not until the Cantonal Government had appointed a commission to take over the control of the property belonging to the village, and quartered on the village six soldiers (who loaded their rifles as they approached Zermatt) that Seiler was eventually admitted to the Burgerschaft on April 7th, 1889, eighteen years after he had made his first application.

The fascinating thing about Switzerland is the variety of its social structures and the attractive element of peasant oligarchy in an otherwise democratic country. The Englishman who is interested in the subtler nuances of Swiss local government will find few books and few Swiss who can inform him. What, for instance, is the difference between a Burger and a Bürger? Of the Swiss I have asked, 99 per cent. showed mild surprise at the question being raised. One per cent. hazarded some sort of explanation. The most plausible of such explanations I quote with considerable reserve. The Burger is a member of the Burgerschaft which owns the grazing rights. Burgers are descended from the original settlers. The Bürger, on the other hand, bears the same relation to the Burger as a modified " ü " bears to the genuine hundred per cent. " u." He is a kind of inferior citizen, a *Beisäss-Bürger*, as he is still, I believe, called in Obwalden. *Beisäss* means " sitting by." The *Beisäss-Bürger* " sat by " the seats reserved in church for the Burgers. The Bürger can vote for, or be elected to, the Gemeinderat, but he cannot obtain admission to the Burgerschaft.

PART II

THE CONTEMPORARY SCENE

Chapter X

BRUDER KLAUS' COUNTRY
(The Brünig Pass, Sachseln and Sarnen)

1. The Brünig Pass

O F the many approaches to Central Switzerland the
Brünig Pass (3,317 ft.) is by far the loveliest. The
finest half-day motor tour in the Alps leads from
Interlaken along the shores of the Lake of Brienz, to the
Haslital, and thence via the Brünig Pass to the lakes of
Lungern and Sarnen and the lake of Lucerne, a run of
45 miles, or 50 if you make the short, and worthwhile,
détour to Meiringen.

The Brünig Pass, the frontier between Protestant Berne
and Catholic Unterwalden, was crossed by the Words-
worths in 1820. Wordsworth was travelling with his wife
and his gifted sister, Dorothy, whose *Journal of a Tour on
the Continent* (1820) was reissued by Macmillan in 1941 in a
scholarly edition of all her Journals, edited by the late E. de
Selincourt.

Here is Dorothy Wordsworth's impression of Catholics
in Unterwalden:

> The picturesque accompaniments of the Roman
> Catholic religion—the elegant white chapels on the
> hills; the steady grave people going to church, and the
> cheerfulness of the valley had put me into good humour
> with the religion itself: but, while we were passing
> through this very hamlet, and close to the mansion of
> the godly man (Mr. M. having lost the cork of a little
> flask) I asked the guide to beg or buy us another at one
> of the cottages, and he shook his head, assuring me they
> would neither give nor sell anything to us *Protestants*

87

except in the regular way of trade. They would do nothing for us out of goodwill. I had been too happy in passing through the tranquil valley to be ready to trust my informer; and (having first obliged him to make the request) asked myself at two respectable houses, and met with a refusal, and no very gracious looks.

I quote this passage as the only example I know in Alpine literature of Swiss Catholics looking askance at English Protestants, but in 1820 the Catholics of Unterwalden were suspicious of English Protestants because they assumed that they would sympathise with the Bernese Protestants, some of whom had recently attempted to invade Catholic Unterwalden by way of the Joch Pass. The memory of civil wars in which religion served to exacerbate Cantonal rivalries was still strong, and the shape of the civil war to come between the Catholic and Protestant Cantons was apparent even in 1820.

Dorothy Wordsworth was a worthy representative of that fine type of Anglicanism which, while rejecting what they believe to be the errors of Rome, find themselves in sympathy with many aspects of the Catholic Church. Of her host and hostess at Giswil she writes: " He and his wife performed their offices to us none the worse for their religion, and notwithstanding my recent experience of Roman Catholic churlishness I looked with no illwill at their little gaudy image of the Virgin." And a little later at Sarnen she exclaims, " In our rambles on foot, how thankful have we been to the Roman Catholics for the open doors of their churches."

Dorothy Wordsworth's Journal deserves far more attention than it has received from mountain lovers. The mountain anthologies of Spender, R. L. G. Irving and my own first anthology contained no extracts from her work, and yet few descriptions of mountain scenery are more evocative than hers.

Three miles from the summit of the Brünig we reach the

lake of Lungern (2,475 ft.), one of the loveliest of Swiss lakes in summer. In spring the level of the lake is lowered, for the water has been drained to supply electric power during the winter and ugly shelving terraces of gravel and sand divide the lake from the green grass, but in summer it deserves the discerning tribute paid to it by an early Victorian traveller, John Hogg, who crossed the Brünig in the early years of the nineteenth century.

Passing through the lovely valley, and by the lake of Sarnen, I saw that *bijou*—the small, but most enchanting of lakes—the Lake of Lungern—of which the water is of an exquisite blue, transparent, and truly *splendidior vitro*, it is surrounded by, or as I will rather call it, set in, mountains of the loveliest and most pleasing forms, clothed with delicious verdure, and at its southern extremity is seen that snow covered Alp—the Wetter-horn, erecting its lofty pinnacle in vivid contrast with the rich green of the mountains below it, and the deep and azure sky above it. This scene, though less sublime than some I had witnessed, yet perhaps exceeded all I had experienced in extreme beauty. . . .

The road now descends about 800 vertical feet to Giswil, whence a path (with Stations of the Cross) leads in an hour and a half to the Sakraments-Kapelle (3,336 ft.) near a spring credited with healing powers. Four miles farther on we come to Sachseln on the lovely lake of Sarnen.

2. Bruder Klaus

Under an altar in front of the high altar of the church of Sachseln rest the bones of St. Nikolaus von der Flüe, who was canonized in 1947. St. Nikolaus was born in 1417 and for fifty years he lived the life of a prosperous peasant farmer, taking an active part in the public life of his Canton. His wife, Dorothea Wyssling, who was also from Sachseln, bore him ten children. In 1467 Bruder Klaus resolved to become a hermit. He was attracted by the idea of a retreat in the distant Black Forest, but he had walked no farther than Liestal near Berne, when the memory of his native hills became irresistible and back he came to Sachseln. The hermitage where he spent twenty years of his life is to-day a place of pilgrimage. It is situated on the slopes of the Ranft above the ravine which leads into the Melchtal. Flüeli-Ranft (2,450 ft.), a quiet holiday resort near the hermitage, is just under three miles from Sachseln. For twenty years St. Nikolaus lived in a little cell, his only nourishment being the Sacrament. Whether you admit the possibility of such deviations from the ordinary course of nature depends on whether you are prepared to believe that higher (or lower) powers sometimes produce supernormal effects in this world of sense experience, and this is not a question which it would be suitable or proper to discuss in this book. But meanwhile those who join the pilgrims who pass between the black marble columns of the little church of Sachseln to pray before the mortal remains of St. Nikolaus may be disposed to agree with St. Augustine that miracles are, as Our Lord seems to have implied, a regrettable necessity. " If you will not believe Me, believe Me for the very works' sake " (St. John x.38). " God's marvels," as St. Augustine says, " whereby He rules the universe have grown cheap, because they go on all the time, so that hardly anyone condescends to notice the wonderful and astounding works of God in any and every seed and grain. So, according to His mercifulness, He has reserved to Himself certain things that He might do, aside from the customary flow and scheme of nature so that men for whom daily matters had grown cheap, might stand amazed when they saw not what was greater but what was *rare*. For a greater marvel is the governing of the whole universe than the filling of 5,000 with five loaves," or, for that matter, the nourishment of St. Nikolaus with the Sacrament alone.

Bruder Klaus (Klaus is, of course, a contraction for Nikolaus) is venerated by all Swiss, Protestant no less than

Catholics, for he is a symbol of that Swiss genius for compromise and conciliation which alone has preserved this mosaic of different races from disruption.

The closing years of the fifteenth century was a period when the concept of nationalism was beginning to weaken the international ideal of a united Christendom. At the very period when French nationalism found a symbol in St. Joan of Arc, the concept of Switzerland was beginning to emerge in the confederacy of Cantons which had just inflicted a resounding defeat on Burgundy. The disappearance of this middle kingdom with its attractive blending of French and German culture entailed disastrous consequences for Europe, the whole history of which might have been very different had there been a buffer state between France and Germany. Meanwhile in Switzerland the victorious Cantons, united in face of the common enemy, relapsed into particularisms when that enemy had been defeated. The inevitable disputes over the spoils of victory were aggravated by the increasing tension between the towns and the pastoral Cantons. The peasants of the Forest Cantons were accused of stirring up the peasants of Entlibuch against Lucerne and Unterwalden. Bruder Klaus' own Canton, Unterwalden, which had supported the peasants of the Haslital against Berne, was accused of being particularly active in such incitements. Now Bruder Klaus was wise enough to realise that the towns were destined to play an important rôle in the young Confederation and that somehow or other a *modus vivendi* had to be found between town and country.

At the Diet of Stans in 1448 Bruder Klaus effected a reconciliation between the opposing parties. A saint in armour saved France at much the same period that a saint at a round table saved Switzerland.

The canonization of Bruder Klaus provoked some misgivings among the simpler Catholics who felt that it was all very well for celibates to become hermits but Bruder Klaus, with his ten children, ought to have stayed at home. To which, of course, it is sufficient to reply that he took this step with the full approval of his wife, who was well provided for, and that he himself could have appealed to those sayings of Our Lord in which He insists that there are occasions when a man may be called on to leave his wife.

The Protestants faintly resented the canonization which somehow seemed to have created a kind of holy curtain between Bruder Klaus and the Protestant Swiss. Bruder Klaus, so they felt, was not the private property of the Catholics, a view with which the Catholics, of course, would be the first to agree. Certainly Bruder Klaus may be described as the Patron Saint of Swiss neutrality. " Don't meddle in foreign quarrels " was the burden of his advice to the Confederates.

The recognition (to which every Christian is *ipso facto* committed) that the routine of Nature is from time to time modified or reversed by supernatural agencies imposes the obligation to examine possible natural explanations before admitting the possibility of a miracle. And it was in accordance with Catholic tradition that the good Bishop Hermann of Constance should have been filled with doubts when rumours of Bruder Klaus' miraculous fasts came to his attention. He accordingly deputed his Suffragan, Bishop Thomas, to visit Bruder Klaus and report on these strange happenings. Not only the laity, he pointed out, but priests were making pilgrimages to this Bruder Klaus. " But the obvious presumption," wrote the good and perplexed Bishop, " is that there is an element of ambition and deceit in all these manifestations." " *Ambiciosa et fallax.*" In other words the Bishop thought that the whole affair sounded very phony, and it was therefore necessary to intervene at once lest " the simple sheep of Christ should be misled." Bishop Thomas visited the hermit and asked him which he considered to be the greatest virtue. Bruder Klaus answered "obedience." Whereupon the Bishop produced bread and wine, which he had brought with him, and commanded Bruder Klaus to partake of them. Bruder Klaus cut the bread into three small pieces and with great difficulty swallowed a small piece and drank a mouthful of wine and was all but sick. The Bishop was duly impressed and reported in due course to Bishop Constance that there was nothing *ambiciosa et fallax* about the hermit or his fasts.

Others were not so easily convinced. Father Durrer of Sachseln who prepared the evidence for the process of canonization told me that for thirty days and nights all the approaches to Bruder Klaus' cell were carefully watched by his enemies who believed that he was being fed in secret. Before he retired to his cell he had been not only a man of substance and standing in his Canton, but also a judge. On one occasion a poor peasant who had mortgaged his land and then wished to redeem it brought a suit against a rich peasant who preferred to retain the land rather than have the mortgage redeemed. The unjust judges found for the rich peasant, and Bruder Klaus, being in a minority of one, resigned his judgeship. It was his indignant colleagues who set the watch on his cell.

The Pope, in his Bull of Canonization, refers to the traditional belief that Bruder Klaus lived for years nourished only by the Sacrament, but does not commit the Church to this belief, which Catholics are free to accept or to reject. I am not convinced by those who maintain that one cannot reject this tradition without accusing Bruder Klaus of fraud, for the evidence that he himself made this claim, though strong, is not coercive. The Bishop of Constance's letter instructing his Suffragan to report on these alleged fasts is in existence, but Bishop Thomas's report on his investigations is not. One thing, however, is certain. Bishop Thomas consecrated the chapel near Bruder Klaus' cell which he would certainly *not* have done had he not been convinced that there was nothing *ambiciosa et fallax* about Bruder Klaus himself.

In any case, whether Bruder Klaus was or was not nourished exclusively by the Sacrament seems to me a question of minor importance compared to the influence which he was able to exert as the result of his sanctity. Men are sometimes influenced by reason and converted by argument, but most people are more readily influenced by example than by dialectics and where the rational approach is reinforced by sanctity the result is all but irresistible. The career of King Louis IX of France, St. Louis, provides many examples of this fact. Bruder Klaus was a great statesman. He could advance the soundest of political arguments on behalf of the policies which he advocated but those arguments would probably have failed had not those to whom they were addressed been impressed by the complete disinterestedness and holiness of the man who made them.

This hermit living apart from the world was gifted with political genius of a very high order. France had conquered and absorbed Burgundy, and Austria was only waiting for the Confederates to quarrel among themselves to absorb Switzerland. I have already described the events which led up to the Diet of Stans, the quarrel over the spoils of war, and the increasing tension between towns and villages. Here is the story of his intervention as described in the *Diebold-Schilling Chronicle*.

On the night of December 21st, 1481, Father Heini am Grund, priest of Kilchherr zu Stans, realised that war between the Confederates was inevitable if things were just left to take their course. He left that evening, rode and walked through the night till he reached Bruder Klaus' cell and next day, just as the Diet was breaking up, Father Heini burst in upon them, bathed in sweat, and begged them to meet again to take counsel with Bruder Klaus, who had accompanied him to Stans. The results of that intervention were all that the good priest could have desired. Bruder Klaus' constant warnings to the Confederates to avoid foreign entanglements was the direct cause of the resistance of Schwyz and Unterwalden to the demands of the French king to whom they were under contract to supply regiments.

Bruder Klaus was, as I have said, the Father of Swiss neutrality. After the crushing defeat of the Swiss at Marignano in 1515 a poet of the people recalled Bruder Klaus' advice to his compatriots:—

> " *Wernd ir daheimen pliben,*
> *bei kinden und bei wiben*
> *hotten die küe uusirlben*
> *ziger und anken gmacht . . .*
> *bruder Claus in seim leben,*
> *hat euch den rat nit geben*
> *gefolgt hett ir im eben,*
> *ir werent nit so weit*
> *gezogen in fremde streit!* "

In other words, had they stayed at home with wife and children and looked after their cows and followed Bruder Klaus' advice, they would not have been involved in far distant wars.

Zwingli, in his campaigns against foreign service, often cited the authority of Bruder Klaus " *den ouch bruder Claus von Unterwalden vorgseit hat.*"

3. The church at Sachseln

Bruder Klaus is buried in Sachseln. There was a church of St. Theodule on the site of the present church as early as 1234. Of the old Romanesque structure the tower alone survives. Bruder Klaus' first grave was in the shadow of this ancient church. Thousands of pilgrims visited the grave and a dispute between the parish priest and the municipality as to the ownership of the gifts which they left, and the offerings which they made, was terminated in favour of the parish priest, and used to build a new church. The foundation stone of the new church was laid by the Papal Nuncio on June 12, 1672. The marble was transported from the quarry in the Melchtal which can be seen from the point where the cable-railway to Melchsee-Frutt begins. The great columns were slowly and with immense labour rolled down the mountain side over a prepared surface of tree trunks, and the polishing was entrusted to the women of the Canton.

In the right transept of the church you can still see on the wax-work figure of the saint the hand-woven worsted smock which Bruder Klaus wore. This passed into the immediate possession of his eldest son, and was eventually given to the church by the family. The rosary is not contemporary, for Bruder Klaus' rosary was distributed to his relations and friends after his death.

In the left transept you can see the famous *Betrachtungstafel*, which was said to have been painted at the request of the hermit and to represent one of his visions. The authenticity of this tradition has been called into question. The church contains in the south aisle the oldest picture of Bruder Klaus. It is believed that his son, whose resemblance to his father was startling, was the model for this painting. Incidentally, a lineal descendant of Bruder Klaus who lives just above Sachseln bears a striking resemblance to his great ancestor.

The bones of Bruder Klaus are encased in the bronze reclining figure of the Saint on his own altar just behind the communion rails. You can just see the end of the fibia bone if you peer through the glass case just inside the bronze feet.

Father Durrer showed us the treasures of the church which are kept in a safe, the gold piece which Bruder Klaus received as pay when he fought in the battle of Ragaz, a crucifix, and monstrance in which Saints Theodule and Mauritius and Catherine and St. John the Evangelist are on the lower tiers and Bruder Klaus alone in his glory at the top. This was rather more than the Papal Nuncio could bear, for the Church had given no official recognition at that time to the popular cult of Bruder Klaus, but all his efforts to have the statue removed were in vain, as was testified by Kaplan Joachim Eichorn.

Bruder Klaus' first burial place was just outside the church, and was covered in 1488 by a figure of the hermit carved in sandstone which was soon so damaged by the pilgrims that a new figure in harder material was placed above the grave in 1518. Both figures can to-day be seen in the little chapel above the empty grave.

Towards the end of the sixteenth century the grave was roofed in. In 1600 a small chapel was built over the grave and the wall separating the chapel from the main church was opened. After the rebuilding of the church this chapel, which still exists, became an entirely separate building. This little chapel is full of ex-votos, amongst others the painting of the storm-tossed vessel in which a company of Swiss in the service of the Duke of Lottringen were nearly wrecked.

In 1732 the bones of Bruder Klaus were transferred to the main church.

The Hotel Kreuz near the church is a historic building. The lower stories are substantially the same as they were in 1489, the year before Colombus sailed for America. An old votive painting of the hotel still hangs in the main lounge. It depicts the fire which destroyed the top stories of the hotel from one of which a man dives head-first (instead of jumping feet first) but was saved in spite of this contempt for the technique of emerging from burning buildings by the intercession of Bruder Klaus and St. Francis, who can be observed in the top right-hand corner. Note in this picture the stream which flows down the same artificial channel to-day as it did in 1656. Bruder Klaus, by the way, seems to have specialised in putting out fires. He is credited with having extinguished a conflagration which threatened to destroy Sarnen.

In the lounge of this hotel there are two very interesting stained-glass windows. The one on the right-hand side (1656) was presented to Niklaus Götsche by the Diet of which he was a member when he rebuilt the top stories of the hotel. The left-hand glass is less interesting. The central part was added later. It shows the arms of the Britschgi family. The family of the founder of the hotel died out in the last century with the exception of one daughter who married the grandfather of the present owner, Herr Britschgi. It is interesting to reflect that for nearly five centuries this historic inn has been managed by the descendants of the man who built it.

4. Sarnen

Sarnen, at the northern end of the lake, the capital of Obwalden (the western sub-canton of the Canton of Unterwalden), is a charming little town. The town hall was built in 1729–31 by Georg Urban. It contains portraits of the magistrates of Obwalden since 1381. The Pfarrkirche, dating from 1739, is the work of Franz and Johann Singer. Johann Singer, either alone or in conjunction with Jacob Singer, built the churches of Cham, Schwyz and Wolfenschiessen. The Friedhofkapell has " one of the loveliest late-Gothic carved and painted wood-ceilings in Switzerland " (Dr. Jenny). There is a charming description of Sarnen in Mr. John Russell's *Switzerland*. He writes:

> The other houses round the square are of many periods, but they bear an unchanging family face; no matter whether they are four hundred years old or were built yesterday, they live together in amity. Lettering, whether Roman or Gothic, does not disturb the rhythm

BROTHER
KLAUS'
ALTAR
at Sachseln

ENGELBERG IN WINTER

K. Meuser, Engelberg

of steep-pitched long eaved roofs (often descending more than half-way to the ground), shutters closed against the noonday sun, and between every house a glimpse of green beyond. To the north there stands upon an eminence the Schutzenhaus. Built as an arsenal in 1752, this exquisite building is now as pacific as the rest of the landscape. It is one of many examples in Ur-Schweiz of the way in which white (if it be " furiously white," as Leibniz suggests) can be a positive force in landscape design. One cannot exaggerate the brilliance of this little fortress, with its elegant central block, armigerous and saddle-backed; its flanking, single-storeyed wings, each crowned with a cupola and black onion; and the dazzling zigzag of its shutters.

Alpnach-Stad, five miles beyond Sarnen, is the starting-point for the Pilatus railway and a steamer station in the Alpnach Bay of Lucerne.

The church (1812–1820), like its contemporary at Kerns, was built by Joseph Singer, the architect of many Lucerne buildings, such as the Mint building in the Mühlenplatz, the Provost's house adjoining the Hofkirche and the Albertis Haus near the Reussbrucke. Joseph Singer was a Vicar of Bray among architects, adjusting himself without difficulty to changes in fashion, Louis XVI, Classic and Empire. At Knutwil near Sempach there is an Empire Church by Joseph Singer not far from the church of classical design which he built at Triengen.

Chapter XI

STANS AND ENGELBERG

1. Stans and Stansstad

THE steamer calls at Stansstad, which can also be reached by car over the bridge which divides the Alpnach Bay from the main lake. Stansstad was the scene of a primitive naval battle in 1315 (see page 40).

It is a short walk from Stansstad to Stans, the capital of the small sub-canton of Nidwalden. It was at the Diet of Stans in 1461 that St. Nikolaus von der Flüe reconciled the warring factions. In 1798 Stans was the scene of a terrible massacre. Revolutionary France had imposed upon Switzerland the Helvetic Confederation, which put an end to the existing inequalities between nobles and peasants, and between the various states and subject territories of Switzerland. The innate conservatism of the Catholic Cantons was incensed by these reforms. Schwyz, Uri, and Unterwalden accepted them only after a spirited though ineffective attempt at resistance (see page 55). Nidwalden continued to resist. The French general Schauenbourg attacked the half-canton both from the lake and from the direction of the Brünig, and made contact with the Swiss in the meadows round Stans, where the inhabitants, some 30,000 in number, fought with the courage of despair. Women and children hurled themselves into the fray. Every house outside the town was burnt, and Stans itself narrowly escaped the flames.

It was at Stansstad that Wordsworth gave a lively demonstration of the fact that it is unwise to assume that poets in general and idealists in particular can be cheated with impunity. At Herzogenbuchsee, for instance,

Wordsworth spent the night in the " Char " rather than pay six francs for a bed.   At Stans the driver demanded twenty-seven francs instead of the agreed eighteen francs, and refused to surrender the coats and cloaks of the party, which he " had locked up in a seat of the Char " till they paid.   The ladies naturally were far more distressed at the prospect of losing their cloaks than of yielding to extortion, but Wordsworth, after assuring the " carman " that " if justice were to be had in Switzerland, he should feel the weight of it," bundled his party into a boat for Lucerne, where he laid a complaint against the errant carman, and pursued the matter with such energy that the coats and cloaks were returned and the carman sentenced to a month's imprisonment.   " We hastened down," writes Dorothy, " to congratulate the conquerors, and give them due praise for the spirit which had carried them through the business, honestly confessing that we, by being willing to submit to imposition, rather than run the risk of losing our coats, should have betrayed our own countrymen, and not done our duty to the Swiss."

Stans is an attractive little town.   Among the things worth seeing are the famous statue of Arnold von Winkelried (page 42) and a historical museum in which a contemporary print of the French attack on Stans should not be overlooked.   In 1791 Nikolaus Purtschert, who built the classical churches at Buochs and Beckenried, built the Breitenhaus in the style of Louis XIV.   Many of those who were killed in the resistance to the French are buried in the churchyard.   The Stanserhorn, a famous viewpoint, is reached by cable railway from Stans in about fifty minutes.

2. Engelberg

The road from Stans to Engelberg passes Wolfenschiessen of which the Parish Church (1775-7) was built by J. A. Singer.   Near the church you can see the wooden blockhouse where the magistrate Konrad Scheuber, a grandson of St. Nikolaus von der Flüe, lived. Thence the road and rail climb steeply to the valley of Engelberg.

The Canton of Unterwalden is divided, as the reader will have discovered by now, into two sub-cantons, Obwalden and Nidwalden. The Obwaldeners and the Nidwaldeners are fully in accord on the evident proposition that the Canton to which they both belong, Unterwalden, is in every way a model Canton, vastly superior to any other Canton, but on the relative merits of Obwaldeners and Nidwaldeners there is a difference of opinion. Engelberg belongs to Obwalden, but is entirely cut off from the Obwaldeners, an island of the elect surrounded by Nidwaldeners. The Nidwaldeners are firmly persuaded that the French invaders in 1798 were guided to the little pass, a mere ridge in the plain which leads from Obwalden into Nidwalden, by a peasant from Obwalden. I have crossed this little ridge and an army which needed a local guide to find this, the one obvious gap, would have been stopped at the frontier of Switzerland, but the legend is firmly embedded in the racial memories of the Nidwaldeners. I mentioned it to a citizen of Stans with whom I entered into chance conversation. He showed no surprise that a wandering Englishman should have heard this story, for, of course, all the world knows how the gallant defenders of Nidwalden had been let down by the traitor of Obwalden. He spoke of this incident as if it had happened quite recently.

The Titlis (10,164 ft.) dominates the valley of Engelberg. It was climbed in 1744 by four local peasants, perhaps the first purely sporting ascent (with no ulterior scientific motive) of a moderately high Alpine peak.

The Benedictine Abbey, which is said to possess the second finest organ in Europe, was founded in 1120, and rebuilt after a disastrous fire in 1729. Until 1798 the valley was subject to the rule of the Abbot. According to legend the angels sang while the foundation of the Abbey was being laid. According to others, the founders chose this spot because it was a place haunted by happy spirits whose melodies could be heard while the Abbey was being built. Dorothy Wordsworth writes:—

> It is no wonder that such traditions are believed by some of the good Catholics even to this day; for never was there on earth a more beautiful pinnacle for happy spirits than the Rock of Engelberg, as we first beheld it, gilded with the beams of the declining sun. Light clouds, as white as snow, yet melting into the thinnest substance, and tinged with heavenly light, were floating around and below its summit. We exclaimed, " There you see the wings of the Angels." Our recollections of that moment cannot be effaced, and some time afterwards my brother expressed his feelings in the following little poem.

The poem in question, *Angels' Hill*, is reproduced in Wordsworth's *Collected Poems*.

3. An Eighteenth-Century Whig visits Engelberg

One of the first eminent Englishmen to visit Engelberg was an enterprising eighteenth-century traveller, Archdeacon William Coxe. At a time when travelling was neither safe nor comfortable, he travelled extensively in Russia, in Sweden and in Denmark, and paid four prolonged visits to Switzerland in the years 1776, 1779, 1785 and 1786.

Coxe was an acute observer of the contemporary scene. A member of the famous De Salis family spoke to me in terms of high praise of his chapters on the Grisons and, in particular, of his scholarly discussion of the Romansch language. As a historian, his Memoirs of the great Duke of Marlborough and of Robert Walpole are of great historical value, and no historian, until recent times, had access to a greater range of unpublished documents and family archives.

In religion, as in politics, Coxe was a firm believer in the *via media*. He detested dictatorship and distrusted democracy. It is, of course, only in comparatively recent times that Englishmen have used the word " democracy " in any but a derogatory sense. When Mr. Gladstone introduced his Bill for extending the franchise in 1866, he was careful to *deny* any democratic bias. " You will exclaim," he protested, " that ' this is democracy.' I reply that it is no such thing." My father was a great admirer of Gladstone, and brought me up in the pure milk of liberalism, but I never heard him speak about " democracy."

One of the things which astonished Coxe in Switzerland was that the democratic Cantons were well governed. " These little states, notwithstanding the natural defects of a democratical constitution may justly claim a large share of our approbation." A result which he attributed to the fact that the evils of democracy were largely counteracted by the medicine with which he was very familiar— " aristocratical corruption." In religion he was for the *via media* between popery and dissent. He did not like the Catholics but he disliked still more the Swiss pietists, samples of whom he met at St. Moritz. They reminded him of the Methodists. They " employ so much time in prayer as to neglect their ordinary business." The Archdeacon, we may be sure, was never guilty of such foolishness.

Coxe visited the Benedictine Monastery at Engelberg. As a Whig, he was naturally perplexed by the Benedictine combination of hierarchy with profound respect for the dignity of the humblest member of Christendom and he was therefore very surprised to find himself dining in the same room as the servants. " The company at table consisted of the Abbot, five or six Benedictines, ourselves, and our servants who, according to the custom of the place, sat down at the same hospitable board as their masters. This intermixture of society, the politeness of the worthy abbot, and the facetious cheerfulness of one among the fathers, rendered the repast as agreeable as it was uncommon." Coxe seems to have been more surprised than displeased by this survival of a Feudalism which, while maintaining distinctions of Office, permitted a far easier social intercourse between people of different rank than in Hanoverian England, where the lines of division between rich and poor were infinitely more rigid than they had ever been in the old Europe.

Coxe was one of the first Englishmen to appreciate mountain scenery. His descriptions of Rosenlaui, the Urner See and Engelberg reveal a genuine appreciation of mountains, glaciers and alpine lakes. Here for instance is a charming little vignette of the valley of Engelberg. " Having issued from the dark forest, we descended for a little way, and unanimously broke into an exclamation of surprise and delight, as we suddenly looked down upon a picturesque plain of an oval shape beautifully wooded, watered by several lively streams, enclosed within a circle of gentle hills, and terminated by a majestic amphitheatre of ' cloud-capped alps '."

4. Engelberg and the English

In recent times the relations between Engelberg and the English have been more than cordial, particularly in ski-ing. It is curious to reflect that the English, who had to travel five hundred miles in pursuit of the various varieties of alpine sport, were largely, but not entirely, responsible for the development of mountaineering as a sport. The English invented the Cresta run at St. Moritz. Curling is a Scottish game, ice hockey a Canadian sport. In ski-ing we were the first to insist that the proper way to test downhill ski-ing is to race downhill. The Alpine peoples blindly copied the Scandinavian form of race, a long distance race, uphill, downhill and level, and instead of setting race courses down their mountains, forced competitors to race along the valley floors. The Slalom, a race down a course defined by flags, set so as to test a competitor's power to turn, is, in its modern form, an invention of the present writer.

In 1930 the Swiss Ski Championship included for the first time a downhill race, the challenge cup for which was presented by the Ski Club of Great Britain. Also, thanks to Herr Adolf Odermatt, that great friend of British ski-ing, a ladies' race was included and for this event the Kandahar Ski Club presented a trophy. Before the race our ladies' team lunched at the hotel near the Trübsee. I was interested to observe the ladies surreptitiously putting small coins into an offertory box connected with the chapel. I gathered, as a result of discreet investigations, that an average of five centimes represented their conception of an adequate supernatural insurance. I therefore added a franc with the result that Miss Doreen Elliott became the first Swiss Open Lady Champion, an honour later won by Miss Jeannette Kessler (now Mrs. Oddie).

Engelberg is a wonderful ski-ing centre, and among my happiest memories is that of a lovely easy tour from Engelberg across the Joch pass to Meiringen after the ladies' race at Engelberg, a tour which is described in my book *Mountain Jubilee*.

In winter the Trübsee lake above Engelberg is a featureless expanse of snow. In summer the stroll round this blue mountain tarn is one of the most charming walks in the Alps. Engelberg in summer is popular not only with mountaineers but also with the aged, who appreciate the variety of level walks which the flat valley bottom provides, and also with parents, for Engelberg makes a special effort to cater for small children.

Chapter XII

MELCHSEE-FRUTT

1. The Lake

MELCHSEE-FRUTT (6,295 ft.) can be reached by car in little over an hour from Sachseln, or by post car from Sarnen to Stockalp and thence by cable-railway. It is, by the way, time that we produced an English equivalent for the word *téléférique*.

During the second world war Melchsee-Frutt formed one of the strong points in the Alpine *reduit*, to which the Swiss army would have retired had Switzerland been invaded. The cliffs near the hotel were blasted to provide bomb-proof shelters for ammunition and food. The slender broadcasting tower, a reminder of those days, may perhaps serve the function for which it was erected in the not so distant future.

In winter Melchsee-Frutt is a famous ski-ing centre. There is good ski-ing till the late spring. There are some fine northern runs down to Stockalp for those who like to do their climbing by cable railway and a great choice of runs on north slopes for those who do not mind climbing.

I fell in love with Melchsee at first sight and as the car which was taking me back to Melchsee from Sachseln rounded the last curves I knew that *la potenza del antico amore* had lost none of its power.

I am writing these lines on a balcony of the Hotel Reinhard overlooking the lake. It is evening and light mists shot with prismatic colouring have softened and subdued the austerity of the Glockhaus cliffs. The Glockhaus, " house of the bells," takes its lovely name from a famous echo, for which it is well worth while to climb the little hillock underneath the Glockhaus cliffs.

Cowbells and the Angelus awaken their appropriate response in this " house of bells."

The Melchsee panorama owes its charm to many factors, partly perhaps to the contrast between the long recession of the Titlis range and Erzegg ridge, and the uncompromising gauntness of the Glockhaus and Hohenstollen precipices. I remember sitting on our balcony puzzled by the fact that there was something in this view which seemed to recall by remote association the lagoons of Venice . . . *remote* association indeed . . . and then suddenly it came to me. Just as the black Gondolas provide the perfect foil to the polychromatic loveliness of the Lagoon city, so the aggressive negation of the colour in the dark Glockhaus cliffs reinforces the blended colours of the lake in which the rich green of the lower slopes is mirrored and reversed, while in the east the iridescent tints of the Titlis snows melt into the blue distances of an Alpine sky. And there was something else which reminded me of Venice. Just as the Salute gathers up and concludes the legato movement of the Grand Canal so the poise of the Hohenstollen provides the perfect finale to the sweep of mountains from the Titlis in the east past the diminuendo of the Erzegg ridge to the crescendo of Rothhorn and Glockhaus.

It is difficult to suggest the sense of space and freedom in this place. There are no fences to confine the walker. He can wander where he will. It was delightful to watch the children undressing near the shore and plunging into the lake which might have been built for children, so very gentle is the shelving shore. One of the loveliest high-level walks in the Alps with the minimum of climbing is the path which leads from the lake to Tannen Alp (6,500 ft.), little more than 200 feet above Melchsee. Thence a rather steeper path leads down to the Engstlen Lake (6,076 ft.). In the eighteenth and early nineteenth centuries one of the most popular of Alpine routes led

from Interlaken across the great Scheidegg, via Grindelwald, to Meiringen and thence via this gem of a lake to
the Joch Pass and Engelberg.

Reckon one hour 45 minutes (an easy two hours in the
reverse direction) from Melchsee-Frutt to Engstlen Lake
and thence in about an hour and a quarter to the Joch
Pass (7,265 ft.) whence you can descend to Engelberg by
chair-lift, cabin-lift and funicular, returning the same
evening via Stans and Sarnen to Melchsee-Frutt.

Another delightful easy walk is to take the path to
Tannen Alp and turn left just before you reach the summit
of the pass and then follow the green ridge to the Erzegg
(7,140 ft.) or even farther to the Balmeregghorn (7,444 ft.).
This is one of the prettiest ridge walks in the Alps, with
glorious views of the Rhone glacier mountains and the
Bernese Oberland and the ravine of the Gental below.

2. A Memorable Day

As a boy I knew the names and heights of the most
obscure Oberland peaks, that is, of peaks which the
mountaineer would deign to recognise as such, but distant
mountains overshadowing valleys which I had never
visited only interested me if they were the kind of mountain
which would be mentioned in the *Alpine Journal*. From
the heights of the Faulhorn range I often saw the Glockhaus
and Hohenstollen, but just as many of those who visited
Berne in past centuries were content to refer vaguely to
the distant " Alps " and never bothered to distinguish
individual summits such as the Jungfrau or Wetterhorn,
so the individual summits of this minor range meant
nothing to me. And yet the range had its own intriguing
appeal. Behind that range, as I knew, was a lake, and
not only a lake but a valley, the Melchtal, and the Melchtal
was something more than a name to one who had been
taught in childhood to honour Arnold von Melchtal,
founding patriarch of the Swiss Confederation.

In more recent years I had come to associate this range with the memory of April dawns seen from the windows of the Kleine Scheidegg. Many a time have I woken just as the Glockhaus began to define its character against the first wash of pink in a sky from which the stars had not wholly fled. Slowly this Glockhaus skyline acquired the challenging magic of a range whose " other side " was a secret, a teasing secret which evoked a faint dissatisfaction every time that the Glockhaus rose beyond the intervening hills. And gradually I came to see that I must explore the other side of my " sunrise range," if my enjoyment of Scheidegg dawns was not to be marred.

On an August day in 1949 I set out to climb the Hohenstollen, sometimes called Hochstollen (8,150 ft.), just under 2,000 feet above the Melchsee-Frutt.

A short climb brought me to an enchanting little tarn, a tarn which had borrowed the darkness of the great cliffs which overshadowed it. I was reminded of Cader Idris' Lyn Cae. Instead of following the bridle path round to the right, I took a short cut up a steep gully. There was one point, and only one, where it was convenient, but not really necessary, to use my hands, and just as a familiar scent or an old tune will reveal the past with the clarity of a landscape at night suddenly disclosed in a blinding flash of vivid lightning, so that momentary contact between rough limestone and finger tips scattered the years like dust and stabbed me with regret for the craft which I can no longer practise.

The gully was steep and exhausting but the short cut was repaid by the glory of the sudden disclosure as I scrambled into the skyline.

The panorama from the Hohenstollen is approved with a star by the passionless verdict of omniscient Baedecker and, perhaps, if as many people visited Melchsee-Frutt as Lucerne, the panorama from the Hohenstollen would be as famous as the panorama of Pilatus. It has grace no less than grandeur, the lyrical beauty of the lakes, the light green-blue of Brienz melting into the dark blue of Thun, forming a perfect foil to the glacier world of Susten, Rhone and Oberland.

Men climb mountains for many reasons, for the joy of conquest (a motive which of course does not arise in the case of easy walks such as the Hohenstollen), for the view from the summit and also for the added interest of the view of the mountains from the plains. One of the moments to which a mountaineer looks forward during a difficult ascent is the moment of relaxation in the valley when he can study with reminiscent pleasure the labyrinthine ways through which he ascended to the ultimate crest. And even in the case of easy walks such as the Hohenstollen the link forged by a climb is of enduring value, for something of one's past life enters into those patterns of rock and ice and snow and green cattle alps which somehow add up to a wholly satisfying unity.

I have often seen the " sunrise range " since then, from the Scheidegg or from the waters of Brienz or the shores of Thun. The range is now resolved into separate and successive peaks. The " other side " is no longer an unsolved mystery, but its appeal is all the more poignant because of the nostalgic memories of Melchsee-Frutt, which are evoked every time I see the sunrise range in the eastern sky beyond the Great Scheidegg or beyond the blue expanses of Brienz.

3. Other Melchsee Memories

Why " Frutt " ? Frutt is an abbreviation of *fruchtbar* (fruitful). Every one of the many " Frutts " scattered throughout the Alps marks the highest point which is " fruchtbar " for cattle. Melchsee-Frutt evolved as a tourist centre, from the hospitable instincts of Herr Reinhard, the grandfather of the present proprietor of the Hotel Reinhard. Herr Reinhard was one of the leading

men in the Canton in which, among other offices, he was
Ober Richter, of which the nearest English equivalent is
" Chief Justice."

Herr Ober Richter Reinhard spent his summer months
in a small alp chalet on Melchsee-Frutt. Owing to his
position in the Federal Government Herr Reinhard had
many contacts with leading people in other Cantons, and
he often asked the children of his friends to spend some
weeks in his chalet at Melchsee-Frutt. Their parents,
in turn, invited the Reinhard children and Frau Reinhard
in consequence was faintly self-conscious about the contrast
between the pastoral simplicity of the alp chalet and the
comfortable and well-appointed homes to which her
children were invited. So the Ober Richter was persuaded
to convert the simple alp chalet into something more
ornate. The additional rooms enabled him to entertain
more children and inevitably the parents of these children
soon began to insist that they must at least pay the bare
costs of their entertainment. And thus in the course of
time a modern hotel, the Hotel Reinhard, built on a site
of its own, developed out of the hospitable instincts of Herr
Reinhard, Ober Richter of Obwalden.

In the front hall of the Hotel Reinhard hangs a map,
dated 1767, which would seem to have been compiled by
memory after a walking tour in the Alps. Engelberg, for
instance, is wildly misplaced. The map provides interesting evidence of that popular canonization of Bruder
Klaus which anticipated the official canonization at Rome.
His cell on the Ranft is indicated in the map. " *Hier hat
St. Niclaus gewohnt und* 19½ *Jahr ohne meschliche Speis und
Trank gelebt.*" (Here St. Niclaus lived, and for nineteen
and a half years existed without human food or drink.)
On the same wall, and near to the map, is a genealogical
tree of which Herr Reinhard is very proud for few can
boast, as he can, of a double line of descent from a canonized
Saint. It is not very easy to trace a single line of descent

back to a Saint, for Saints with families have a quite exceptional rarity value.

I asked Frau Reinhard whether the family had been to Rome for the canonization. They had not. Indeed they were not very enthusiastic about the official canonization. In my many talks with Frau Reinhard I was often reminded of Father Martindale's remark, " Catholics use up all their available unity on points of defined dogma, and have nothing left over for anything else." Frau Reinhard, for instance, takes her dogmas from the Church but claims the right to form her own opinions on things which have not been defined and, as she is a lady of great culture, wide reading in philosophy, and marked independence, her Catholicism is at once orthodox and very individual.

" I can sympathise," she said to me, " with Swiss Protestants who feel as if they had been robbed of Bruder Klaus by the official canonization, for our Swiss Protestants have an immense reverence for Bruder Klaus and they feel that he belongs to them as Swiss and not only to the Catholics."

" But surely," I said, " no Catholic would dispute that."

" No, but the feeling remains, the feeling that the Church was trying to monopolise a great Saint who belonged to Switzerland, Catholic and Protestant. After all, we did not need the canonization at Rome to convince us that Bruder Klaus was a saint. We've all known that for centuries.

" He was not only a saint but a genius, a man of the most versatile attainments. He knew about war from first-hand experience, as an officer, about politics from first-hand experience as a politician, about farming as a farmer. He seems, however, to have realised that the world is far more influenced by sanctity than by arguments. He had to withdraw from the world to influence the world, and to find in solitude and in prayer the supernatural force which he needed to reinforce the arguments drawn from political experience."

4. O Lobä, Zuä Lobä

On the evening of our return to Melchsee-Frutt we walked along the lake to the little chapel. The last wave of colour was ebbing from the Titlis snows and the lake was in deep shadow. Suddenly we heard from a neighbouring alp the ancient hymn to Our Lady which the herdsmen sing as the light fades. Here is the hymn they sing, first in the dialect, secondly as translated into high German:—

O lobä, zuä lobä, i Gott's Namä lobä !
O lobä, zuä lobä, i iise-rä liäbä heiligä
*   Fraiwä Namä lobä !*
O lobä, zuä lobä, i allä liäbä Heiligä
*   Gottes Namä lobä !*
God und d'r liäb heilig Sant Antoni
Sant Wendel und Sant Marti,
Und d'r vilsälig Landesvater Bruäder
*   Chlais*
Wellid disi Nacht hiä und uf dieser Alp
*   Herbärg ha !*
B'hiät God Seel, Veeh, Liib, Ehr und
*   Guäd,*
Und alls, was uf disi Alp g'heerä tuäd.
O lobä, zuä lobä, i Gods Namä lobä !

O lobet—zu loben !—In Gottes Namen
*   lobet !—*
O lobet—zu loben !—In uns'rer lieben
*   Frauen Namen lobet !*
Gott und der heilig sant Antoni und
*   sant Wendel,*
Und der vielseliger Landesvater Bruder
*   Klaus*
Die wollen heut' Nacht auf dieser Alp'
*   die lieb Herberig halten !*
Behüt' Gott Seel', Ehr', Leib und Gut !
Und Alles, was hier auf diese Alp gehört
*   und ist !*
O lobet—zu loben !

And here is an English translation:

Oh give praise, in the name of God give praise!

Oh give praise, in the name of Our dear Lady give praise!

May God and holy Saint Anthony and Saint Wendel and Saint Martin

And the very holy brother Klaus give their sheltering protection tonight to this alp!

May God protect soul and honour, body and possessions

And everything which is and belongs to this alp!

Shortly after leaving Melchsee-Frutt I climbed the Wildgerst with my son Peter. The rose of the sunset had withered on the Wetterhorn as I limped down past the last of the cow-sheds of my beloved Grindelalp. No places on earth could mean more to me than Grindelwald and Grindelalp, but one thing was needed to round off the perfection of this hour of mountain peace, the herdsman's hymn:

O lobä, zuä lobä, i Gott's Namä lobä.

MELCHSEE-
FRUTT

Titlis in the
background

Franz Schneider,
Lucerne

THE JESUIT CHURCH, LUCERNE

Franz Schneider,
Lucerne

Chapter XIII

THE TOWN OF LUCERNE

1. Introductory

" OF the ancient architecture and most expressive beauty of the country," writes Ruskin, " there is now little vestige left; and it is one of the few reasons which console me for the advance of life that I am old enough to remember the time when the sweet waves of the Reuss and Limmat (now foul with the refuse of manufacture) were crystalline as the heaven above them; when her pictured bridges and embattled towers ran unbroken round Lucerne and when the Rhône flowed in deep-green softly divided currents round the wooden ramparts of Geneva."

It is only too true that the vandals of the Industrial Revolution destroyed more beauty than the bombers of the second world war. But although Switzerland has lost much of its ancient beauty, much remains.

The Schweizerhof Quai occupies the space where the wooden bridge ran continuously from the Kappelbrücke (which still survives) to the steps of the Hofkirche, and Ruskin, who mourned the vanished bridges, inevitably regarded the Schweizerhof Quai as a modern outrage. But the Quai was old when I was young and therefore I have never been able to think of it as a modern *arriviste* gate-crashing into an ancient setting. On the contrary, it is associated in my mind with those charming old coloured prints of the 'forties and 'fifties. One of these prints I can recall, as I write—in the background a primitive lake steamer with an enormous elongated funnel, in the immediate foreground an English paterfamilias, period 1850, complete with side-whiskers and a top hat, helping his wife to alight from a dignified barouche. Ruskin's father might have served as a model for this travelling Englishman.

The Schweizerhof has evolved with the years and adapted itself to changing fashions, but no modernisation can destroy its period charm. It was here that Wagner completed *Tristan* in September, 1859. The Schweizerhof still retains the flavour of a world that is dead, the world in which Russian Grand Dukes and Austrian Archdukes were not impoverished exiles but the most desired of guests, guests whose staple beverage was champagne. If their ghosts still walk the Schweizerhof corridors at night, I hope they will not be disturbed by the mocking laughter of the Yankee iconoclast, Mark Twain, who spent a few nights at the Schweizerhof during his " tramp abroad."

Ruskin was a mediaevalist, but even Ruskin might have grudgingly conceded that some nineteenth-century inventions can be turned to good purpose, had he seen the mediaeval embattlements of Lucerne floodlit while the kindly night censored all the modern buildings which Ruskin hated. The effect is as if the spirit of modernity were doing penance for all her unlovely disfigurements of the earth by throwing into radiant relief the legacy of beauty which the nineteenth-century vandals failed to destroy.

Modern Lucerne is proud not only of the fact that it is the Mecca of tourists of modest means, but also an Athens by the Reuss, a cultural centre with a famous music week. The Art museum near the station acquires on loan every year a succession of modern and mediaeval masterpieces.

In the eighth century a Benedictine Monastery was founded on the site of what is now the Hofkirche, but it is almost certain that the earliest settlements date from long before the eighth century. The actual foundation of the 'town with its encircling walls dates from the end of the twelfth century. Lucerne's great importance derived from the fact that the town was the crossing point of two important trade highways—the St. Gotthard and the road from the Oberland across the Brünig to Zug and Zürich.

On November 7th, 1332, Lucerne signed an alliance with the Forest Cantons which had defeated the Habsburgs at Morgarten and on July 9th, 1386, Lucerne and her allies defeated Leopold III of Habsburg at the little Lake of Sempach, ten miles from Lucerne.

2. The Hofkirche

Let us begin our exploration of Lucerne with the Hofkirche. Of the old church, which was burnt in 1633, little remains but the Gothic towers. The interior is an attractive blend of Gothic and Renaissance. The church contains an impressive Gothic crucifix dating from the end of the fifteenth century and two remarkable side altars, the death of Our Lady in the style of the Upper Rhine school (fifteenth century) and a lovely Pietà probably of a slightly earlier date. In the Pietà the broken and tortured body of Our Lord is Gothic in feeling, but the expression on the Madonna's face suggests the dawning influence of the more naturalistic schools of the Renaissance. The Madonna of this Pietà seems to me transitional, mainly Gothic in feeling, but foreshadowing the dawn of a very different tradition. You should not leave without seeing the St. Michael in the chapel by the main entrance and the late-Gothic carving of the Apostles in the Garden of Olives. This theme has been particularly popular in Lucerne ever since Pope Sixtus IV, in 1480, gave the Lucernois the privilege of including the Apostles on the Mount of Olives in their city banner. As a result, this motif is to be found in many private houses as well as in chapels, as for instance in the sandstone relief on the south wall of St. Peter's chapel in Lucerne.

3. Lucerne North of the Reuss

Near the corner formed by the modern bridge and the north bank of the Reuss is the Haus zur Gilgen, an ingenious blend of the old Gothic tower with eighteenth-century architecture. We cross the bridge and turn left down the Kapellgasse at the entrance of which stands a modern Swiss bank on the site of the home of a sixteenth-century Mayor of Lucerne who employed Holbein to decorate the interior and the exterior of the house with a series of frescoes. The vandals of 1824 destroyed this house without provoking the slightest protest, and frescoes which would have attracted lovers of art from all corners of the world, vanished as decisively as if they had been destroyed in a full-scale air bombardment.

St. Peter's chapel, from which the Kapellplatz takes its name, dates from the twelfth century and is the oldest church in Lucerne, but it has been ruined by many disastrous restorations. The sandstone relief of the Mount of Olives on the south wall, which has already been mentioned, is attractive. The fountain in the front of the church is a modern copy of a mediaeval fountain.

The Kapellgasse leads into the Kornmarkt, in which the most important building is the Rathaus which dates from 1600, on the first floor of which there is a museum containing, among other interesting exhibits, several banners captured at Sempach, the coat of mail of the defeated Duke Leopold, Roman bronzes and a collection of stained glass of the fourteenth century and some charming thirteenth-century stone reliefs from the monastery of St. Urban.

The Weinmarkt, which is a few yards from the Korn-markt, was the centre of old Lucerne. The old Rathaus was situated in the south-west corner of the Weinmarkt until the end of the fifteenth century. It has been transformed into a Weinstube, and the paintings on the walls still recall its past glories. The fountain is a copy of a fifteenth-century fountain, the original of which can be seen in the Ritter Palace (see below).

From the Weinmarkt we change direction and turn sharp right and then left into the Hirschenplatz where the pig market was held until the middle of the sixteenth century. Its modern name is derived from the Hirschen Inn. Of the old inn little remains but the beautiful iron-work sign. Goethe spent a night in the Adler Hotel near by.

The Hirschenplatz leads into the Mühlenplatz, which was the Mayfair of Lucerne in the eighteenth century. Facing us, as we emerge from the Hirschenplatz, is a fine specimen of the patrician houses of old Lucerne, the Haus Göldlin von Tiefenau. Near this house was the old Nunclature.

It was in the Mühlenplatz that the wife of General Ludwig Pfyffer held her Salons at which patrician officers, on leave from foreign service, used to meet. The " Generalin," as the General's wife was called, was buried in 1780. On the following night, a robber opened the coffin in search of jewels whereupon the Generalin sat up and protested loudly. She returned to her house clad only in her shroud and lived for twenty years without ever smiling again.

It was in front of General Pfyffer's house, the Lucerne centre of ardent supporters of the French monarchy, that the symbol of the French Revolution was planted by Vinzenz Rüttimann, the son of a Burger, who had recently been admitted to the exclusive ranks of the patriciate. Under the Napoleonic régime Rüttimann the younger maintained a Salon for supporters of the revolution. His services were appreciated by Napoleon and he became, in succession, Mayor of Lucerne and the President of the governing body for Switzerland (Tagsatzung). When Napoleon fell he won the confidence of the Bourbons by the swiftness with which he repudiated his revolutionary past, and defended aristocratic tradition. He ended his career as the acknowledged leader of the aristocratic party, which had resumed its control of Lucerne.

Don't leave the Mühlenplatz without a glance at the Munz, a charming eighteenth-century house in the north-west corner.

4. Lucerne South of the Reuss

Now let us explore the south bank of the Reuss. Starting from the station we walk down the Bahnhofstrasse, past the theatre, to the Jesuit church. The Jesuits played a great rôle in Lucerne from the seventeenth century to the outbreak of the Civil War in 1847. Their enemies greatly exaggerated their influence in the controversies which led to the Civil War and the victorious Protestants passed a law which has never been repealed, exiling the Jesuits. A few Jesuits are tolerated in Switzerland but any attempt to legalise their position would still provoke opposition.

It would be an interesting experiment to lead a Catholic into the church and tell him that the church was Benedictine. If he was reasonably well-informed he would point indignantly at the altar and the absence of a choir to confute you. The Jesuits are not a religious Order, but a " Society," " the Society of Jesus," and whereas the primary purpose of the Benedictines is the recitation of the Sacred Office in choir, the Jesuits, like secular priests, recite their office in private, and consequently do not need a choir. The Jesuits are not monks withdrawn from the world. Their purpose is to maintain contact with the world of sinners, and leaven its pagan resistance to the " hard sayings " of Our Lord. For them the Mass is not only a holy sacrifice which can be equally well offered far removed from the sight of men, but a divine drama to be enacted, when occasion lends itself, with all possible splendour, in full view of the entire congregation. The dominating position of the altar in this church, and its glorious proportions, have clearly been designed for this end. The Jesuits have always understood the hunger of simple people for pageantry. In Italy they were among the first to exploit the appeal of Baroque architecture to that theatrical element in the Italian temperament which revels in Grand Opera. Similarly, they delighted the Lucernois by processions far more colourful than a modern Lord Mayor's Show. These attained a climax of splendour when St. Francis Xavier, the Apostle of the Indians, was acclaimed patron of Lucerne in 1654. The citizen chosen for the rôle of St. Francis rode in triumphal procession through Lucerne, in a chariot similar to the chariots of Roman Senators. The chariot was drawn by negroes. Dragons and devils danced round the chariot wheels, and the conquered walked, as in Roman triumphal processions, behind the victor's chariot, but in this case the conquered were not kings and chieftains but the personifications of the vices—lust and ambition and worldliness. Little boats covered in green branches floated like islands in the lake, and demons climbed out of the Reuss on to floating platforms to raise mock storms which were calmed when St. Francis cast his cross into the river. Meanwhile the thunder of cannons and the music of church bells awoke echoes in the surrounding hills.

The memory of this pageantry survives in the painted vault, in the centre of which we see St. Francis riding in triumph through the heavens in a chariot drawn by a somewhat ill-assorted team consisting of an elephant, a giraffe and a leopard. Since Saints do not blow their own trumpet, an angel has been enlisted for this purpose and, through a long slender trumpet, he proclaims that St. Francis is the protector of the town (that is Lucerne) and the region. A little cherub seated in the chariot empties a cornucopia of blessings on the assembled multitudes below. Well, perhaps multitudes is hardly the right word, for the admiring spectators seem to be drawn exclusively from what would be described in the States as Lucerne's "Social Register." A bishop, surrounded by noblemen, raises reverential eyes to the passing chariot.

The Mount of Olives theme so popular in Lucerne (see page 117) reappears in a seventeenth-century painting by Lanfranco on the altar. Do not leave without seeing the charming stucco decorations on the wall of the sacristy.

The former Jesuit College, now the State Record Office, faces the Government buildings (Regierungegebäude), formerly the Ritterschen Palace, which takes its name from Lukas Ritter. Lukas Ritter was a talented careerist who had begun life as a saddler and risen to the rank of Colonel in the service of France and, on his return, had been elected Mayor of Lucerne. "He desired," writes Herr Xaver von Moos,* "to demonstrate, by the Palace which he proposed to build, that he was interested not only in power but also in beauty. He employed an Italian architect who combined an immense admiration for classical ideals with a secret conviction, not only that the world was shortly coming to an end, but also that he was a reincarnation of the prophet Elias. It was, he believed, his particular mission to rescue mankind from damnation by pronouncements both cryptic and apocalyptic." Lukas Ritter, a man of strictest orthodoxy, was unimpressed by his prophetic pretensions and instigated proceedings on a charge of heresy, with the result that the unfortunate architect was condemned to death. As this pseudo-Elias was being led to the place of execution, past the house in which Ritter was confined to his bed by a severe illness, he called out to his accuser and challenged him to substantiate his accusations before the eternal judge in the valley of Josaphat. Next day his accuser was dead.

Of Ritter's heirs none were willing to make themselves

---

* *Luzern Ein kleiner kunstführer*. Published by Joseph Stocker, Lucerne. I am indebted to this admirable and beautifully-illustrated book for much valuable information.

responsible for the debts incurred with the result that the town had to complete the Palace of which only two stories had been built.

The influence of the Florentine Renaissance is unmistakable in the rusticated façade which is so reminiscent of the Palazzo Strozzi. Both buildings are products of the Renaissance, but of that rebirth of classical ideals which is supposed to have produced the Renaissance there is little evidence, either in the Florentine or Lucerne Palaces. Ritter's Palace has far more in common with the Gothic towers which rise from the battlegrounds of Lucerne than with Paestum or the Parthenon. The fascinating renaissance chimney-piece on one of the upper floors recalled the decorative themes in the Miracoli at Venice but is no more evocative of the classical feeling than a Bellini Madonna of the Nazareth in which Jesus grew to manhood.

The original of the Weinmarkt fountain is preserved on the ground floor of this Palace. It is incidentally of interest to note that the Gothic style lasted for a century longer in churches than in secular buildings. Compare, for instance, the lower stories of the Ritter Palace with the nave of the Franciscan church, both of which were built in the sixteenth century.

The Franciscan church is a few minutes' walk from the Ritter Palace. The choir dates from the end of the thirteenth century and the nave from the sixteenth century. An admirable fifteenth-century fresco depicting the Crucifixion fills the great space over the arch leading into the choir. The pulpit (1628) by Nikolaus Geissler, and H. V. Räber's St. Louis in the choir (1651), are fine examples of late Renaissance, but by far the most charming feature of the church is Our Lady's chapel, the late Gothic structure of which blends harmoniously with Baroque ornamentation (*circa* 1620).

The banners painted on the walls of the nave are copies

of banners captured in the battles at Sempach and in the
Burgundian Wars. The original banners once hung in
the church but were removed to the Rathaus museum in
1622 and replaced by paintings. Of the original banners
only five remain. The French invaders of 1798 are
alleged to have removed those that are missing.

Many fine examples of the stately homes of the old
Lucernois aristocracy still survive. Nearly facing the
Cantonal library (which is just north of the Franciscan
church), you will find the Haus von Segesser. Or again,
walk in a southerly direction down the Obergrundstrasse
which passes the west end of the Franciscan church, cross
the Pilatus Platz, and you will pass on your left the old
Himmelreich (1772), now the Konservatorium. A little
farther down you take the turning to the right, just before
the church, and you will find yourself in a few minutes in
front of the handsome Schloss Steinhof.

One of the most charming of these old buildings is now
used for the Lucerne library (the staff of which have been
most kind and helpful to me in my researches). This was
originally the Sonnenbergsche Haus and was built about
1674. It is situated on the Reuss-steg just beyond the
Reussbrücke. In the old days there was no Reuss-steg
road between the building and the river, and the door,
which was built to provide an entrance from the Reuss-steg,
spoils the symmetry of the Renaissance façade. The floor
of the main hall was raised two feet, which slightly spoils
the proportions, but it is a lovely building for all that, with
some charming stucco decoration.

5. The Famous Bridges

The Kapellbrücke is adorned with about a hundred
rather indifferent paintings representing episodes in the
history of Lucerne, and in the life of St. Leodegar, the
patron saint of the city. These date from the early
seventeenth century, and have recently been restored.

The bridge was an important part of the town's defence system. Facing the lake, from which the attack would come, the parapet is higher than on the side of the river.

The paintings on the Spreuerbrücke, a seventeenth-century version of the Dance of Death, are of far greater interest. I am impressed by Mr. Xaver von Moos' suggestion* that Meglinger's paintings are evidence of a strong reaction against the pagan elements of the Renaissance, a reaction for which the Catholic revival of the seventeenth century was responsible. The Renaissance rejoiced in the overflowing vitality of a brilliant and creative age. Never before had life seemed so inexhaustible in its resources and possibilities. And as the certainty of an infinitely greater happiness in the world to come became clouded by doubt, Renaissance men were more and more reluctant to face the fact of death. The knights in Gothic tombs are represented in the sleep of death, their hands crossed on their breasts, awaiting the Resurrection, but there was an increasing tendency in the Renaissance to represent the departed not recumbent but erect, not in death but in the full vigour of life. The tombs in the Frari at Venice illustrate very clearly the contrast between the Gothic and Renaissance treatment of death. In Meglinger's Totentanze, Death is no longer the Nihilistic destroyer of all human values, but a messenger whose mission it is to lead men from the passing pomps of the world to the timeless beauty of the next. The knight in the most attractive of the Spreuerbrücke series is not paralysed by horror as he meets Death. He retains his composure and casts one last lingering glance of affection on the beauty of the world which he is leaving. The Gothic Totentanze was intended among other things to scare the worldling into penitence. A favourite theme was that of Cardinals or secular princes snatched with violence from the pomp and pageantry of this life and projected into the

* *Op. cit.*, p. 102.

presence of the supreme Judge, but the knights and fair
ladies of Meglinger's Totentanze pass from life with a grace
and dignity as if they had long prepared themselves for
death.

It is interesting to contrast Meglinger's treatment of the
Totentanze theme with Jacob von Wyl's Totentanze
(1615) in the Regierungsgebäude. Von Wyl is Gothic in
his choice of subject, but Renaissance in his treatment of
silks and embroidery. His Kaiserin might have ordered
her robes from Veronese before her encounter with Gothic
Death.

There is no mistaking the gusto with which von Wyl
paints his skeletons but the figure of Death in Meglinger
has a faintly perfunctory air, as if he had been introduced
pro forma into a theme which was not of the artist's choosing.
Meglinger has far more in common with Dutch and late
Italian masters of the genre, Giorgione for instance, than
with von Wyl, and he is happiest and most himself when
he is interpreting the lyrical loveliness of pastoral scenes
and romantic fairy-like landscapes.

There is nothing as interesting as the Spreuerbrücke
paintings in the Kunstmuseum, but there is a fine Crucifixion by an unknown Gothic master, some interesting
works by sixteenth-century Lucerne artists, Diebold
Schilling and Martin Moser, and representative works by
nineteenth-century Swiss artists, notably Robert Zünd.

6. Wagner and the Villa Tribschen

The Villa Tribschen is situated on a little promontory
on the south shore of the lake and can be reached in a
twenty-minute walk from the railway station along the
Inseliquai and Alpenquai. It was in this Villa that
Wagner composed the *Meistersinger*, began *Siegfried* and
completed the *Ring*. He lived here with Cosima von
Bülow from 1862 to 1872.

Supreme geniuses are often supreme egoists. Wordsworth

and Wagner are cases in point. Aristotle somewhere says that friends should be cultivated as carefully as apple trees. Wagner's method was to shake the branches till every possible apple had fallen to the ground and then complain loudly that the tree wasn't doing its duty. At the age of fifty-one the region once occupied by friends was a devastated area. But, as in Wordsworth's case, whenever things looked really desperate the fates would intervene. In the case of Wordsworth a sinecure would fall vacant or a relation would conveniently die. In Wagner's case the *deus ex machina* was in sober fact if not a *deus* at least a *rex*. Ludwig of Bavaria had resolved as soon as he was king to come to Wagner's rescue, for the Wagnerian world of knights and pilgrims and pinnacled palaces and lakes and dreaming swans was the kind of world which he hoped to create when he ascended the throne. And in point of fact Ludwig did build some very Wagnerian castles in Bavaria, during the years when he was gradually losing his reason.

Ludwig was eighteen when he solved Wagner's financial difficulties, and thereby created his own, for Wagner was fantastically extravagant, never more so than when he was spending somebody else's money. He did not make the slightest effort " to temper the wind to the shorn lamb " which had run up so guilelessly to the shearer's hand. The unworthy reluctance of the politicians to allow public funds to be spent on the gratification of Wagner's flamboyant taste and the increasing unpopularity of Wagner with all ranks of society from dukes to dustmen finally rendered his departure from Munich desirable.

The king had solved his financial problems and his friend von Bülow was *invited*, the *mot juste*, to help in the solution of Wagner's matrimonial problems by handing over his wife on loan until such time as Wagner could divorce his own wife and marry von Bülow's. " It clearly suited Wagner's convenience," writes the late Hugh

Kingsmill, " as much to be frank with von Bülow about his future requirements where Cosima was concerned as it suited Hitler's to be frank with Hacha and Schuschnigg about the new domestic situations that had suddenly arisen in their respective countries. Had von Bülow not been apprised of the New Order which was coming into being, there would have been no point in Wagner indicating his place in this order, in the elevated but sufficiently explicit terms of a letter he wrote to von Bülow during his convalescence: ' Her (Cosima's) due is freedom in the noblest sense of the word. She is childlike and profound— the law of her being will always lead her to the highest only. . . . She belongs to a peculiar world order which we must learn to grasp through her. You will have, in the future, more propitious leisure and freedom of your own to consider this, and to find your noble place by her side. And that too is a comfort to me '."*

Ludwig bought the Villa Tribschen for Wagner and he lived there with Cosima for the next six years at the king's expense " and that too, beyond doubt, was a great comfort to him."

It is difficult for those of us who have fallen under the spell of Wagner's supreme masterpieces to understand the fierce opposition which his Operas at first provoked, but perhaps his critics were unconsciously aware of the fact that there is much in his music which heralds the modern Nihilistic revolt against the restraint of that Graeco- Roman-Christian civilisation of which Wagner was at once the child and the enemy. As long ago as 1857, Amiel, the Geneva philosopher, wrote in his journal the following criticism of Wagner's *Tannhauser*:—

> It is music depersonalised—neo-Hegelian music— music multiple instead of individual. If this is so, it is indeed the music of the future, the music of the Socialist Democracy. . . . The overture pleased me

* *The Progress of a Biographer* (Methuen).

even less than at the first hearing; it is like Nature before man appeared. Everything in it is enormous, savage, elementary, like the murmur of forests and the roar of animals. It is forbidding and obscure, because man, that is to say, mind, the key of the enigma, personality, the spectator, is wanting to it. . . . This music has its root and its fulcrum in the tendencies of the epoch— Materialism and Socialism—each of them ignoring the true value of the human personality, and drowning it in the totality of Nature or of Society.

7. The Bourbaki Panorama

Pacifist propaganda has one solid achievement to its credit—the Bourbaki Panorama at Lucerne next door to the glacier garden. This was commissioned by a Society of Pacifists who believed that a realistic representation of the misery of a routed army would be effective propaganda for peace. Unfortunately wars are started by people who have every intention of *inflicting* the miseries of defeat on their opponents, and who would therefore be unaffected by the moral of the Lucerne Panorama. The episode commemorated occurred during the Franco-German war of 1870–1871. General Bourbaki's "Army of the East," broken and routed, was thrust back on the Swiss frontier near Pontarlier. Bourbaki demanded an asylum. A convention was arranged between Bourbaki and General Hertzog, commanding the Swiss army, and on January 31st, 1871, the French army crossed the frontier.

The officers were allowed to keep their swords, but the rest of the army had to pile up their arms. *Les Tronçons du Glaive*, by the brothers Margeritte, contains a vivid description of the surrender:—

The darkness had fallen when the tragic procession began to file through the ravine behind Pontarlier. By the road of Les Verrières and Les Fourges the compact stream flowed and trickled. A confused mob of cavalry, infantry, and gunners moved forward in a dark torrent, dense and continuous. The roar of the cannon and the furious rattle of musketry covered their retreat through the defile of La Cluse.

The Prussians were still attacking. Two of the regiments, " the only troops which had not lost heart," made a half-circle. These, at least, were heroes. For seven hours they tramped through blood and snow, striding over corpses. . . . To a flag of truce, and to the suggestion that he had no choice but to yield, General Robert replied, " Death still remains." Until nightfall the cannon and musketry covered the cross-roads, and the retreat of the artillery proclaimed that even in the hour of disaster honour was not lost. Nearly ninety thousand men had already been thrown on Swiss soil. The tragic procession lasted for two days. The tide flowed on through the defile formed by the Swiss troops, who leant motionless upon their arms. As the French entered they heaped up their rifles and ammunition, their sabres and revolvers, into two enormous piles on each side of the road. Lances stuck into the ground bristled like a leafless forest. Along the whole length of the moving line nothing was heard except a complaining murmur raised by thousands of dry, hacking coughs. And so they limped past, with bleeding and swollen feet, shivering in rags which swarmed with vermin, with unkempt hair and shaggy faces. The inhabitants assembled by hundreds laden with gifts. They wept for compassion. The very poorest gave . . . into great wooden troughs they poured warm milk. Barns and stables were soon full. A boundless charity held out its arms, touched to pity by a flood of horror such as no man remembered to have seen.

Edouard Castre, the Genevese artist, employed as his assistants a whole staff of specialists, and spared no trouble to get all his details correct. The spectator climbs a staircase which leads to a circular platform entirely surrounded by Castre's Panorama, covering an area of 1,330 square metres. Castre's main objective was to produce a life-like representation of the great surrender.

At many points the foreground is continued in plastic relief, a device which we associate with theatrical scenery. Thus a train in the Panorama consists of one real waggon which joins the painted waggons and, so skilful is the transition from the real to the painted carriages, that one is hardly conscious of any difference between the actual carriage and the representation. Children are enchanted by such masterpieces of illusion, aesthetes shudder, but there is a trap for the aesthete who is too indiscriminate in his condemnation. Ask him whether he thinks that the young artist, who painted the Sappers marching at the head of a Bernese regiment, could conceivably have evolved into a great Master. If he replies with a contemptuous sniff you can tell him that those Sappers were painted by the young Hodler, who was sufficiently advanced for his genius to be recognised even by the kind of critics whose main object is not to lose caste with the ultra-advanced.

I confess to a personal bias in favour of this Panorama, for I was shown round it in my boyhood by a veteran of 1871 who had been present with his regiment when Bourbaki surrendered, and whatever be its merits as a work of art, it is certainly a most valuable historic document. This great painting by Castre tells us a great deal about the armies which met at Les Verrières, but there is something in this Panorama which mere coloured photography could not give. Castre was a naturalist, but he had the eye of an artist for composition, and the grouping of his human material conforms to definite standards. Moreover, the artist is master of time, and can synchronise on his canvas, as Castre has done, episodes which in real life did not occur simultaneously. But whatever be the artistic merits or demerits of this vast canvas, the historian, at least, owes a debt which cannot be disputed to the society of pacifists who commissioned the Lucerne Panorama.

J

8. The Glacier Garden

The Glacier Garden is one of the finest relics of the distant ages when the smooth and polished rocks which are now exposed were polished and rounded by the immense ice stream which covered what is now the lake and plain of Lucerne. The giant cauldrons, thirty-two in number, were carved out by rocks which fell through crevasses to the glacier floor, and were swept round and round by glacier torrents.

There is a fine painting in the museum of an imaginary, but convincing, reproduction of Lucerne in the glacier age. The mountain relief of the Lucerne region is interesting as the first of its kind. It was constructed in the middle of the eighteenth century by General Pfyffer. Archdeacon Coxe, who interviewed the General in 1776, tells us that the General took more than ten years to complete the relief. " In the prosecution of this laborious performance he has twice been arrested as a spy; and in the Cantons has frequently been forced to work by moonlight in order to avoid the jealousy of the peasants, who think their liberty would be endangered should so exact a plan be taken of their country."

The Lion of Lucerne, which is carved out of the limestone cliff which rises from a little lake in the Glacier Garden, was modelled by the famous Danish sculptor Thorwalden, and carved out of the rock by Lucas Ahorn of Constanz. It was completed in 1821. It is a memorial to the Swiss who fell in the defence of the Tuilleries, a perpetual reminder of the honourable rôle played by Swiss regiments on foreign soil, a subject which is too important to dismiss in a paragraph, and to which, therefore, I propose to devote the chapter that follows.*

* Strictly speaking, the chapter that follows should have been included in the first part of the book, but I have placed it in the second part because it should be read just before or just after visiting the Lion of Lucerne.

Chapter XIV

THE LION OF LUCERNE

1. The "Zapolotes"

LONG before the Swiss were called Swiss and many centuries before the birth of the Swiss Confederation soldiers of fortune left Helvetia to fight on foreign soil. In the fourth century, according to tradition, soldiers of Schwyz, Hasli and Unterwalden helped to expel the Goths from Rome, and saved the Eternal City. Charlemagne's advance guard when he marched against the Hungarians was largely composed of men from Lucerne. Nowhere was the enthusiasm for the crusades greater than in Helvetia, a term which may conveniently be retained to describe what is now Switzerland at a time when the word " Switzerland " was unknown. Helvetians fought under the Emperors in the plains of Lombardy, and the professional backbone of the army which defeated the Habsburgs at Morgarten was probably composed of soldiers who had seen active service under the Hohenstaufens.

If you ask a Swiss whether he knows how the Swiss flag originated he will reply indignantly, " Every Swiss knows that the Swiss flag was originally the flag of Schwyz," but if you continue, " Yes, but how did Schwyz get their flag ? " the odds are a thousand to one that he will hastily change the subject. It was in 1289 at the siege of Besançon that fifteen hundred volunteers from Schwyz decided the issue of a hard fought fight. Rudolf of Habsburg was so impressed by their gallantry that he had a white cross sewn on to their red banner, and thus instituted what was later to be the national flag of Switzerland.

The Forest Cantons round the shores of Lake Lucerne, the nucleus of modern Switzerland, defeated the Habsburgs, as we have seen, in the three battles of Morgarten, 1315, Sempach, 1386, and Näfels, 1388. The successful resistance of these peasant communities to the onslaught of Austria provoked as great a sensation in the fourteenth century as the Battle of Britain in 1940. The pattern of these victories against Austria, in the second of which Duke Leopold III of Austria lost his life, was repeated in the three battles between the Swiss and Charles the Bold of Burgundy. The Duke was defeated at Grandson, near Neuchâtel in February, 1476, and again at Morat in June 1476; and lost his life in the battle of Nancy where the Swiss, fighting in alliance with the Duke of Lorraine, inflicted a final and crushing defeat on the forces of Burgundy. In Eastern Switzerland Maximilian of Austria was defeated in the battle of Calven and forced to make peace in 1499.

As a result of these victories and in view of the fact that the Swiss, thanks to national service, could put 80,000 first-class troops into the field, their military prestige stood so high that Henry VIII sent Sir Richard Pace in 1515 to Zürich to negotiate an alliance with the Swiss League. Pace, who was a friend of St. Thomas More and Erasmus, wrote of the Swiss much as a modern diplomatist might write of an atom-bomb monopoly. He was convinced that a State which gained their active support would dominate Europe. His respect for their valour was balanced by his dislike for their business methods. He admitted that the Swiss kept their bargains, but he insisted that those who negotiated with the Swiss would need to be provided with ample wealth, for the greed of the Swiss was such that they threatened with death any foreign negotiator who was niggardly in his offers. The expenses of such negotiations were increased by the necessity to keep " open house " and to entertain the Swiss on a lavish scale.

The Swiss in foreign service have provoked many

literary invectives of which perhaps the first is the camouflaged attack in St. Thomas More's *Utopia*, camouflaged
because the Swiss are referred to as Zapolotes derived from
a word meaning " Those who sell themselves freely."
The marginal note in the first edition of *Utopia*, *Gens haud
ita dissimilis Elvetiis*, makes it clear that St. Thomas was
referring to the Swiss.

Therefore they hiere soldiours oute of all countreis and
sende them to battayle, but cheifly of the Zapoletes.
This people is 500 myles from Utopia eastewarde. They
be hideous, savage and fyerce, dwellynge in wild woodes
and high mountaines, where they were bredde and
brought up. They be of a harde nature, hable to abide
and susteine heate, colde, and labour, abhorrynge from
all delicate deintyes, occupyenge no husbandrye nor
tyllage of the ground, homelye and rude both in buildinge
of their houses and their apparel, geven unto no goodnes,
but onely to the breedinge and bringynge up of cattel.
The moste parte of their lyvinge is by huntynge and
stealynge. They be borne onelye to warre, whyche they
diligently and earnestelye seek for. And when they
have gotten it, they be wonders glad thereof. They goo
furthe of theire countrye in greate companyes together,
and whosoever lackethe souldyours, there they proffer
theire service for small wages. This is onelye the crafte
they have to gette theire livyinge by. They maynteyne
theire life by sekinge theire deathe. For them whome-
syth they be in wayges they fyghte hardelye, fyerslye,
and faytherfullye. But they bynde themselfes for no
certeyne tyme. But upon this condition they entre into
bondes, that the nexte daye they wyll take parte with the
other syde for greatter wayges, and the nexte daye after
that, they wyll be readye to come backe agayne for a
lytle more moneye. There be fewe warres thereawaye,
wherin is not a greate numbre of them in bothe
partyes. . . . This people fighteth for the Utopians
agaynste all nations, bycause they geve them greatter
wayges, then annye other nation wyll. . . . Nor the

Utopianes passe not how many of them they bring to
destruction. For they beleve that they should doo a
verye good deade for all mankind, if they could ridde
out of the worlde all that fowle stinking denne of that
most wicked and cursed people.

This passage may have influenced subsequent attacks
on the Swiss, such as Thomas Nash's remark in 1594 that
" Law, logicke, and the Switzers may be hired to fight
for anybody."

Perhaps the peak of anti-Swiss invective is attained by
Pope in his *Dunciad*:

Around him wide a sable Army stand,
A low-born, cell-bred, selfish, servile band,
Prompt or to guard or stab, to saint or damn,
Heav'n's Swiss, who fight for any God or Man.

2. The Swiss Regiments in France

On September 14th, 1515, Francis I was watching the
changing fortunes of the battle of Marignano. He had
fought in the front ranks and the dents in his armour were
clear evidence that he had been lucky to survive. The
issue was still in doubt when the army of Venice arrived,
and forced the valliant Swiss to retreat. Marignano, like
Morgarten, was to prove a turning point in the history of
the war. At Morgarten the Swiss had proved that
infantry could defeat cavalry, at Marignano that even the
finest infantry in the world was no match for artillery.
The Swiss had lost the battle but not their honour. " *Je
Vous assure, Madame,*" wrote Francis to his mother, " *qu'il
n'est pas possible de venir avec plus grande furie ni plus hardiment
que les Suysses.*" The King realised that it was better to
have such men as allies than as enemies and on November
21st, 1516, he signed, as we have seen, a celebrated treaty
which served as the basis for all future treaties between the
Swiss countries and France. In 1521 this treaty was
transformed into an alliance. The Swiss agreed to provide
16,000 soldiers if the King was attacked.

This was not the first time that the Swiss had been in the service of the King of France. As early as 1497 Charles VIII had appointed as his personal guard " *Cent hommes de guerre Suisses* " and this *corps d'élite*, the *Cent-Suisses* as they were called, remained in the service of the King for four centuries. When King Francis was taken prisoner at Pavia (1525) he looked with emotion on the dead and dying of the *Cent-Suisses* and said, " If all my soldiers had done their duty like these foreigners it would be you who would be my prisoners."

The battle of Marignano was a decisive date in the history of Switzerland. It marks, as we have seen, the virtual end of Swiss imperial pretensions. Thereforward the military prestige of the Swiss rested on their record in the service of foreigners.

It is misleading to describe all the Swiss in foreign service as mercenaries. There were always Swiss mercenaries, the men who enlisted as *individuals* on their own initiative in foreign regiments, and who thereby severed their ties with their own Cantons and country, but the Swiss who were enrolled as the result of military capitulations between the Cantons and France were no more mercenaries than were the Americans who in 1940 joined the Eagle Squadron which fought so gallantly in the Battle of Britain. The Swiss regiments officially served *à titre d'alliés et d'auxiliaires permanents*. The alliance between France and the Swiss Cantons was an important factor in saving Switzerland from dismemberment, and the Swiss who joined the regiments which fought in France were rendering a great service not only to France but to Switzerland. These men did not regard themselves as mercenaries in the service of foreigners. They fought under their own Cantonal banners. Pride of caste, pride in the splendid traditions of the Swiss regiments and pride of Canton and country were the imponderables to which their chiefs appealed before battle. It was as " loyal and beloved confederates," that is as *Swiss* that Colonel Pfyffer addressed the regiment who protected the King of France from the assaults of the Huguenots during the retreat from Meaux in 1567, and it was his appeal to be mindful of the honour of *Switzerland* which encouraged them to fight on against overwhelming odds. A Swiss regiment was in effect a miniature Switzerland with its own laws and its own courts of justice against which there was no appeal. Burin des Roziers* quotes the case of a Swiss who was arrested by the French for a theft in Versailles but promptly handed over to a Swiss court-martial when the Swiss protested to the King.

The rate of pay and the number of troops to be provided were determined by the military capitulations between the Cantons and foreign powers, and of course the Swiss like other professional soldiers expected to be paid, but *pas d'argent, pas de Suisse* implies that the Swiss alone among all the sons of Adam expect to be paid for their services. In point of fact the Swiss often subordinated their financial interests to their sense of honour. Nobody would suspect Guichardin, the author of *The History of Italy*, of any bias in favour of Switzerland, but he recalls that in 1495 when Charles VII was on the point of denying to the Pisans the liberty which he had promised, it was the influence of the Swiss which shamed him into keeping his word. They declared that they would renounce their pay and their pensions and return the golden chains which he had given them rather than tolerate such a breach of faith. Michel de Castelnau reports that after the Duke de Guise had captured Rouen he gave orders to his troops to return to camp. "Few obeyed other than the Swiss who have always been very disciplined." In some Swiss regiments the theft of a chicken was punished with death.

It was, of course, in the main the influence of their commanders which determined whether the Swiss behaved

* *Les Capitulations militaires entre la Suisse et la France.*

well or badly in the hour of triumph. Sometimes they ran amuck, but on the balance they had far higher standards than other soldiers.

In the seventeenth and eighteenth centuries the Swiss soldier was paid at the rate of eighteen livres per month out of which he had to pay for his food. But the pay was often in arrears. In 1598 the crown of France owed the Swiss for arrears of payment 36 millions of gold livres. In their relations to the Swiss the French did not manifest a high sense of honour, a fact which gives point to the famous retort: " You fight for money," said a French officer to a Swiss, " we fight for honour." " Yes," replies the Swiss, " we both fight for what we have not got."

If the Swiss had not fought for honour as well as for pay many regiments would have been disbanded. Many a Swiss Colonel had to mortgage his estates and some died in extreme poverty because they had paid out of their own pocket the pay owing to the troops by the French King.

The courage of the Swiss regiments was tested in many countries and for many causes. Even more impressive than their valour is the sobriety of the dispatches in which their colonels reported to the Cantons at home. They contented themselves with assuring the " *gracieux seigneurs* " that everybody had done his duty. " By a tacit convention," writes Major P. de Vallière, " no attention was drawn to individual acts of valour. Every man had his share of a common glory. Nobody was entitled to feel any special pride in a brilliant feat of arms for among the Swiss the word soldier was synonymous with courage. In their dispatches no individual is mentioned for gallantry. The names of the fallen are given without any other commentary save ' Killed by the enemy. May God save their souls.' "*

* *Honneur et Fidelité Histoire des Suisses au service ètrangers.* This is the authoritative history of the Swiss in foreign service to which I am indebted for many of my facts.

The religious wars in France provided an exacting test
not only of the courage of the Swiss who fought but of the
honour of the Swiss who had signed treaties with France.
The Prince de Condé appealed to the Protestant Cantons
to provide him with regiments, but the Bernese and the
Genevese authorities, in spite of their sympathy with their
co-religionists in France, refused to dishonour their treaties
with the King of France.   Individual Protestants volun-
teered for service under Condé, and though Calvin depleted
his personal resources to contribute to their pay, the Canton
of Geneva gave no official countenance to the enrolment of
these volunteers.

In September, 1567, Catherine de Medici, alarmed by
the rising power of the Huguenots, secured a promise of
reinforcements from Switzerland.   The Protestant leaders
resolved that the Swiss regiment under Colonel Louis
Pfyffer of Lucerne should be intercepted and routed before
they could join the King, who was with his mother not far
from Rosay.   Rumours of this plot reached the King and
he sent an urgent message to the Swiss who were to have
spent the night at Château-Thiery.   At ten in the evening
Pfyffer gave the alarm.   On the morning of the 28th the
sound of approaching regiments provoked the greatest
alarm at Meaux, which was virtually undefended, and
great was the relief of the King and his court when the
advancing regiment revealed themselves as the Swiss,
who had marched 45 kilometres during the night to
forestall the Huguenots in their attempts to seize the
King.

Early next morning the King and his Court set out
with the escort of the Swiss, the ladies of the Court riding
in the centre of the regiment.   They were subject to
incessant attacks by Coligny's cavalry and infantry, but
only thirty of the regiment failed to reach Paris in safety.
Next day the regiment paraded in front of the King who
conferred upon Colonel Pfyffer the collar of St. Michael.

Pfyffer refused to accept a personal recompense in money so long as his men had not been paid.

Louis Pfyffer was born in 1524 of a wealthy commercial family in Lucerne—his father was a linen merchant. Louis Pfyffer's regiment was famous for its discipline. He was a man of sincere and genuine piety, much beloved by his officers, two hundred of whom paid all their own expenses while fighting with the regiment.

The greatest stain on the reputation of the Swiss in France was the part they played on St. Bartholomew's Eve. Among the assassins of Coligny were two Swiss, Burg from St. Gall and Koch of Fribourg, and though the *Cent-Suisses* remained at the Louvre and took no part in the massacre, many of them subsequently pillaged the homes of the rich Huguenots. The Swiss people, irrespective of religion, were horrified by the massacre. " Catholics and Protestants," writes Captain de Vallière, himself a Protestant, " combined to welcome the fugitives from France."

3. The Swiss Regiments in the Service of Holland and Great Britain

The treaties between the Protestant Cantons and Catholic France withstood the strain of the struggle with the Huguenots, but eventually the sympathies of Swiss Protestants for their co-religionists in France and elsewhere proved decisive.

The Revocation of the Edict of Nantes (1685) had a great influence on recruiting. At Zürich the preachers denounced Louis XIV as Anti-Christ, thereby facilitating the propaganda of those agents of the Protestant powers who hoped to recruit Swiss regiments for service against the aforesaid Anti-Christ. On March 10th, 1690, the five Protestant Cantons and the town of St. Gall signed an alliance with Great Britain, and agreed to supply regiments for service in the Low Countries.

Service in Holland soon proved very popular, particularly in Vaud which had a surfeit of young men of good family whose ambitions were thwarted by Berne, to which Lausanne was subject, for the Bernese reserved the principal administrative posts in Vaud for themselves. The simplicity of life and manners in Holland pleased the Swiss Protestants. The Calvinistic plainness of life had at least the advantage of being economical. The Swiss were struck by the contrast between the simple uniforms in which the distinctions of rank were marked only by the badges of rank, and the expensive ornateness of French uniforms. A captain in Holland had to be content with one horse and one valet, whereas in France a sub-lieutenant would be expected to maintain three horses and a staff of servants, often ruining both himself and his family in the process. Among the Swiss Vaudois who served in Holland may be mentioned the father of Benjamin Constant, the lover of Madame de Staël.

Thousands of Swiss found service under the British Crown. On August 5th, 1883, a memorial was unveiled on the hills of Bushy-Run to Colonel Henri Bouquet of Rolle whose brilliant leadership saved the British colonists in the revolt of the Red Indians in 1764.

The names of famous Swiss families (De Watteville and De Salis among others) appear in the lists of those who raised regiments for the service of Great Britain. Several thousand Swiss served under Louis de Rolle of Soleure, a former officer of the Swiss guard of Louis XVI, as a kind of Marine corps, disembarking from His Majesty's frigates to fight in African deserts, in the forests of America, and in India where the Swiss played a rôle in the capture of Seringapatam. While Swiss were serving the Protestant crown of Great Britain their fellow countrymen fought in the service of the Catholic kings of Spain and Naples. Occasionally the Swiss found themselves opposed by Swiss. After the army of Mayenne had been routed at Ivry the only Swiss who stood their ground found themselves in the presence of the Swiss who were fighting for Henry IV. Both regiments lowered their pikes while the officers in the victorious army implored and obtained from Henry IV permission for the Swiss in the defeated Army to return home with their flags and their arms and personal possessions. At Malplaquet (1709) two Bernese regiments, each of which was commanded by a Colonel de May, members of the same family, fought against each other. In order to avoid a repetition of the mutual slaughter at Malplaquet a special clause was inserted in subsequent military treaties. None the less a similar case occurred at Baylen (1808) in the war in Spain. Such cases were exceptional, though inevitably their number was systematically exaggerated and exploited by those Swiss who were opposed to the capitulations.

4. The Men Commemorated by the Lion of Lucerne

Ignorance has always been the great ally of those who have sought and still seek to belittle the achievements of the Swiss in foreign service. But there is one exploit of the fighting Swiss which shamed even the most rancorous critics into some semblance of uneasy respect, the exploit which is commemorated by the Lion of Lucerne.

It was August, 1792. Those of the Swiss guard who were due for leave preferred to stay and face the dark future with their comrades in arms. Men on leave returned hurriedly and eight veterans on the retired list living in Paris gave their old uniforms a good dusting and stumped along to the Tuileries to die, if need be, with their friends. The Catholics—they were not all Catholics— went to confession and a young lieutenant, Forestier by name, wrote to his family in Switzerland, " If misfortune touches the king, and there are less than six hundred of us dead at the foot of the royal staircase we shall be dishonoured. I would gladly die if this could help to save the unfortunate king." His desires were granted for Forestier was among the six hundred who died.

On the morning of the sixth the King for the last time reviewed the national guard. The mob howled " *A bas le roi*," and many of the French national battalions promptly deserted to the revolutionaries.

The King returned to the Palace, pursued by hostile clamour. His councillors urged him to leave the Palace for the National Assembly and place himself at the disposition of the representatives of the people. The Queen opposed this surrender and urged that honour at least might be saved, but finally yielded to the insistence of the ministers. " If the King goes," said Bachman, " all is lost."

The King went, and the Swiss guard remained, and a wave of discouragement passed through the Swiss ranks. It seemed pointless to resist now that the King had left. One by one the French guards deserted them and went over to the mob. Finally the gunners left. At 9 a.m. there remained only forty Grenadiers, thirty national guards, two hundred French gentlemen and the Swiss.

The leaders of the mob approached the Swiss and urged them to surrender. At 10 a.m. the mob opened fire, and the King heard the sound of the guns. Louis was no coward. He would gladly have given his life for his country, but he was a born appeaser and shrank from the responsibility of sending other men to their death. Shortly after ten he sent Marshal d'Hervilly to the Swiss with an order to retreat to their barracks. D'Hervilly without taking time to read the message attentively hurried off to the Swiss and cried out that the King had ordered them to proceed to the National Assembly. The Swiss were overjoyed by what they interpreted as a command to rally to the defence of the King.

The appearance of a detachment of the Swiss in the Assembly provoked a panic and two left-wing deputies promptly jumped out of the windows. " I do not wish," said Louis to the Swiss, " that men as brave as you should die. Surrender your arms." He confirmed in writing an order which was equivalent to a sentence of death for the Swiss.

De Salis ordered the Swiss to pile their arms. Many wept but they obeyed. *Honneur et fidelité*, but never had the fidelity of the Swiss to their oath been subject to a more cruel test. It was easy to die fighting in defence of the King, but to honour their oath of obedience by surrender to a merciless mob called for supreme fidelity.

The mob had no sooner possessed themselves of the surrendered arms than the butchery began. They were not content to inflict a quick and merciful death upon the Swiss. A Swiss private was instructed slowly to saw the head off his captain. " That fine head will look well on the top of a pike. We must not disarrange the *coiffeur*." The man refused, was promptly massacred, whereupon two obliging women slowly sawed Captain Erlach's head off his shoulders and mounted it on the point of a pike.

Meanwhile the four hundred Swiss in the Tuileries fought on until overwhelmed by the mob, who outnumbered them a hundred to one. When the butchery was over two small Swiss drummer boys aged nine and fifteen were found on the Place du Carrousel weeping on the corpse of their father. " To the death with them," screamed the frenzied savages, and within a few moments they joined their father.

Six hundred Swiss died on August 10th, two hundred were massacred subsequently in the September massacres and only two hundred escaped and returned to Switzerland. Nothing, so wrote Napoleon at St. Helena, in all his life had given him a more powerful impression of a field of corpses than the Swiss who fell at the Tuileries. Lamartine, who was no conservative, paid a notable tribute to the Swiss guard. " These men," he wrote, " with no interest in politics, republicans ready to fight against the republic, faced death not for their beliefs or for their country but for their word of honour. This indifference of the Swiss for the cause of the king or of the people rendered their heroism not more holy but more military. Theirs was not the devotion of the patriot but of the soldier."

This is only a partial truth. Most of those who died at the Tuileries were good Catholics, all were good Christians. They died in defence not only of the King but of Christianity, for the mob which murdered them was the same mob that was to enthrone a prostitute on the altar of Notre Dame. The simplest soldiers in the Swiss guard had infinitely more in common with the Christian King than with the anti-Christian mob. A Catholic from the Forest Cantons had as little sympathy with a Jacobin as a highland Catholic of to-day would have with a Glasgow Communist.

Those Swiss were not the last to fall in the service of a French monarch. In the retreat from Moscow the Swiss regiment continued to fight with their traditional heroism long after most of their comrades had been killed. "In the history of war," writes Major P. de Vallière, "such cases are rare. Only an infantry possessing extraordinary moral qualities can continue to fight after losing 80 per cent. of its effectives." Napoleon fell and the Bourbons returned to the throne of France. France still owed nearly a million francs to the Swiss guard, but the debt was never paid and many survivors of the massacre died in extreme poverty and were reduced to begging their bread. The pensions which the Bourbons had undertaken to pay remained unpaid. But *pas d'argent, quand-même les Suisses* was ever the unavowed mottoes of those who served the King of France and over two hundred Swiss of the reformed Swiss guard died in defence of Charles X during the 1830 revolution.

On August 2nd Charles X abdicated and released the Swiss from their oath of loyalty thereby writing *finis* to

three and a half centuries of devoted, and too often un-
requited loyalty to the French crown. Many of the Swiss
disbanded by Charles X remained on in France and formed
the nucleus of the first regiments of the famous foreign
legion which was founded.

5. The Controversy Provoked by the Lion of Lucerne

The Lion of Lucerne is one of the best-known monuments in the world, and it is a little odd that, in Switzerland,
so few people are aware that a controversy raged round
the dying Lion when the monument was first completed.
Two leading Liberals in Sempach, Gernet and Ruttiman,
complained that the Swiss who fell fighting for their own
country should have priority if monuments were to be
erected. Others complained that the monument should
have been erected in Paris, that the inspiration was foreign,
the designer foreign, and the sculptor foreign. " Nothing
Swiss about it." A certain Professor Wolfgang Menzel
describes the contemporary reaction in his memoirs written
in 1877:

> After the Bourbon Restoration in France, the Lucerne
> aristocrats felt that they needed the support of the
> Bourbons. The outward symbol of this dependence was
> the Lion. . . . It was a fine idea to honour the fidelity
> of the Swiss who died on August 10th, 1792, but this was
> exploited as a reactionary demonstration thereby alienat-
> ing the sympathies of many Swiss. . . . On August
> 10th, 1821, the Lion was ceremoniously unveiled. It
> should have been a National ceremony for all Switzer-
> land, but only the aristocracy took part. They flooded
> into Lucerne from all directions, and the streets were
> thronged by old men in the old-fashioned uniform of
> the earlier Swiss Guard, and by old ladies with green
> spectacles and ugly hats. It was almost as if the court
> of Marie Antoinette had risen from the grave.

The students took no part in the unveiling ceremony.

K

Professor Menzel, the author just quoted, was a student at the time and held a protest meeting at Küsnacht where he expressed the hope that a new William Tell would save the situation. Some enthusiastic democrats even attempted to damage the monument.

The animosity aroused in Swiss Radical circles by the unveiling of the Lion of Lucerne did not disappear. On the contrary the opposition to the military capitulations increased as the years passed. There were no Swiss regiments in France but Swiss regiments continued to fight in Italy for the temporal power of the Pope and for the King of Naples, and the strong and natural sympathy of most Swiss for the cause of United Italy finally found legislative expression when the Federal Government passed a law forbidding Swiss citizens to fight in foreign armies without the express permission of the Government, such permission only to be granted in rare cases where a Swiss was in search of military experience for the benefit of the Swiss army. But even after the enactment of this law in 1859 many Swiss continued to serve as individuals in foreign armies. More than 4,000 for instance fought in the American Civil War, many of them on the side of the South.

6. Advantages and Disadvantages

It was inevitable that the military treaties, so alien to the whole ethos of the nineteenth century, should come to an end. It was clear after 1848 that the system of military treaties was doomed by the *Zeitgeist* of a century dominated by the kind of Liberalism which derived from the eighteenth-century revolt against hierarchy and tradition. The aristocratic tradition of the fighting man was nowhere stronger than in Swiss regiments traditionally recruited by the aristocratic families of Switzerland. The Swiss radicals could not be expected to be predisposed in favour of regiments commanded by men bearing such

names as Pfyffer, von Reding or de Salis.   The Radical
campaign of denigration has had far-reaching effects.
" No, we are certainly not proud of the Swiss who fought
for foreigners," a charming Swiss lady remarked to me.
" They just offered their services to the highest bidder."
A libel, for the Swiss never put themselves up to auction,
and no Swiss regiment ever changed sides under the
inducement of higher pay.   Even where they had every
religious inducement to break the terms of the contract as
in the cases we have cited of the Huguenot approach to
Berne and Geneva, they did not betray their *honneur et
fidelité*.   There are, of course, many Swiss like my friend
who are faintly ashamed of this chapter in their history,
but only because they are ignorant of the chapter in question.   The patrician families whose ancestors raised
regiments for foreign service are not in the least apologetic,
and their pride is shared by the descendants of those who
served in the regiments which the patricians raised.   I
have been shown, more than once, letters received from,
and journals kept by Swiss serving in France or Spain,
and these links with the past are always exhibited with
pride.   In the remoter Catholic valleys you will often see
in Corpus Christi processions peasants wearing the uni
forms of their forefathers who served abroad.   And it was a
Protestant, Major de Vallière, who raised a literary monument to the disbanded legions, a monument more effective
than Thorwalden's monument in stone, as a vindication of
the men commemorated, for this gifted author has convinced his readers not merely that the Swiss regiments
were loyal and courageous, which needed no proof, but
also that they rendered an immense service to the cause of
Swiss independence.   His book sold by tens of thousands
even though the cheapest edition cost eighty francs.   It is
often given as a prize in Swiss regiments, but what is more
significant is the large number of Swiss in comparatively
humble walks of life, policemen, private soldiers and so

forth, who have asked the author to sign the copies which they have bought.

Major de Vallière does not conceal the disadvantages of the system. The Swiss recruiting agents of foreign Powers proved to be both a corrupting and a disintegrating influence. They were handsomely remunerated, and tended to identify themselves to some extent with the Powers for whom they recruited, and to reproduce in Switzerland the conflicts of Europe. Again, thousands of the Swiss who left their country for foreign wars did not return, and most of those who did were unfitted for any useful career in their own country.

Against these disadvantages must be set far greater advantages. It is probable that Switzerland would have lost her independence but for the French alliance, an alliance which endured because the French could not dispense with the Swiss regiments. It was the fear of a French intervention which deterred Austria from attempting to incorporate the Grisons in the Empire. The House of Savoy on the other hand coveted Vaud and the lost city of Geneva, and the certainty that Catholic France would intervene to save Protestant Geneva from being reannexed by Catholic Savoy was by far the most important guarantee for the continued independence of Calvinistic Switzerland.

Foreign service was a perfect school of war for the Swiss, and the fact that the treaties gave them the right to recall their regiments in case Switzerland was attacked ensured that magnificent regiments trained and paid by foreign powers were always available as an army of reserve in the event of an emergency.

Again the military treaties guaranteed to the Swiss great economic advantages. Swiss domiciled in France were exempt from taxes and their merchandise from custom dues.

For many of the Cantons the question of foreign service was not a problem of balancing advantages and disadvantages. It was a case of Hobson's choice. Switzerland in the sixteenth century was grossly overpopulated, a population as great as that of Great Britain being confined into a much smaller area. The only possible emigration was the military emigration. Francis I had no less than 163,000 Swiss in his service. Throughout this period the Swiss serving in France were about a quarter of those serving in foreign armies and the Swiss regiments in France sent back no less than 36 million livres between 1594 and 1605 alone. Zwingli, the Swiss reformer, found it easy, as I have already pointed out, to incite the citizens of Zürich against foreign service because foreign trade provided Zürich with the necessary foreign currency. Foreign service was the recourse of a comparatively small number of individuals, mostly aristocratic officers whose aristocratic pretensions were equally obnoxious to the rising class of bourgeoise merchants and to the artisans. The Central Cantons, on the other hand, who were not self-supporting, and who had to purchase from abroad most of their food, were unimpressed by a campaign which if successful would have deprived them of foreign currency. Zwingli, as the Protestant historian William Martin rightly observes, offered to the men of the Forest Cantons the choice of dying of hunger or enforced celibacy!

It is significant that the Treaties were abolished when Switzerland needed all available labour to obtain her share of the profits of the industrial revolution. Again by a curious coincidence the very year 1859, when the Swiss made service in foreign regiments illegal, also witnessed the publication of *Peaks, Passes and Glaciers*. Switzerland had no sooner ceased to be the recruiting ground of Europe than it became "the Playground of Europe." The foreign currency which in past centuries had been secured by means of foreign service is now guaranteed by the fine quality of Swiss exports and by the attraction of Swiss scenery. Whereas in the past the Pfyffers of Lucerne had raised regiments for the service of the French King it was a scion of the same aristocratic house who built one of the best hotels in Lucerne, the National. But I had the impression when I lunched with Colonel Pfyffer, that the hotel remained a minor interest in his career. Colonel Pfyffer, who as a distinguished officer in the Swiss army carries on the military traditions of his family, showed me with great and justifiable pride not the Hotel National but the old engravings of the retreat from Meaux in which his distinguished ancestor had played so great a part in the rescue of the French King.

7. The Swiss Guard

The only Swiss soldiers still in foreign service are the Swiss of the Papal Guard. The Papal Guard was formed in 1506, and originally consisted of 150 men who had been recruited by Peter von Hertenstein, son of the Mayor of Lucerne, who was also the victor of Morat, at the instigation of Pope Julius II (1503–1513). After a few months of peaceful service the Swiss Guard went into action in the Papal campaign against Perugia and Bologna. The first chapter in the history of the Swiss Guard came to a tragic conclusion on May 6th, 1527. Clement VII, who had ascended the Papal Throne early in that year, though reluctant to incur the hostility either of Charles V of Spain or of Francis I of France, finally decided for the French alliance. The French were decisively defeated at Pavia on February 24th, 1525, in spite of the fact that 14,000 Swiss had fought on the French side. On May 6th, 1527, the Imperial troops entered and sacked Rome. The Swiss Guard were almost annihilated in the Piazza S. Pietro. *Cadunt gloriose Helvetii* was the tribute of Jean Cave d'Orléans. Those who took refuge in St. Peter's were massacred at the foot of the high altar. The only survivors of the 189 Swiss being 42 who were charged with the duty of ensuring the retreat of the Pope to the Castle of Sant'Angelo, where the

Pope remained during the siege which lasted a month. When the Pope finally surrendered, among the hard terms imposed upon him was the complete disbandment of the Swiss Guard.

Twenty years later, during the pontificate of Paul III, the Swiss Guard were reconstituted.

Thirteen members of the Swiss Guard saw active service at the Battle of Lepanto on October 6th, 1571. They had been placed by the Pope at the disposal of Admiral Colonna, Commander of the Fleet, and fought as his bodyguard with great distinction. One of them, Hans Nölly from Kriens on the Lake of Lucerne, captured two Turkish standards which may still be seen in the Museum at Lucerne (see page 118). For little more than two centuries the history of the Swiss Guard was comparatively uneventful. After the French Revolutionary troops had entered Rome on February 10th, 1798, the Papal Guard were disarmed, and only nineteen of them were allowed to leave Rome with Pius VI who died in exile. The Swiss Guard were once again reconstituted when Pius VII re-entered Rome on May 24th, 1814, a few weeks after the abdication of Napoleon. Colonel Louis Pfyffer who had left Rome with Pius VI was charged with the reconstitution of the Papal Guard by Pius VII.

The Pope as a temporal sovereign had his own pontifical troops which must be distinguished from his personal bodyguard, the Swiss Guard. The pontifical troops were disbanded when the temporal power came to an end in 1870. The Swiss Guard remained. No recruit is considered for the modern Swiss Guard unless he is at least 5 feet 9 inches in height. He must be a practising Catholic, and a member of a Swiss Catholic family of honourable reputation. No recruit is accepted below the age of eighteen or above the age of twenty-five, and all recruits for the Swiss Guard must have previously completed their Swiss military service.

The colours of the uniform, blue, yellow and red, date from the pontificate of Leo X (1513–1527) and are the colours of the Medici family of which that Pope was a member. There is no evidence for the common belief that the uniform was designed by Michelangelo. It is possible, perhaps probable, that the design of the uniform was influenced by Raphael. His careful painting of uniforms and ceremonial robes certainly had a considerable influence on the fashions of the period.

Once a year the Swiss Guard assemble to do honour to the memory of those who died in defence of the Pope on May 6th, 1527. The modern monument (1927) by Zimmerman, in the Vatican city, is infinitely less famous, and perhaps less deserving of fame than the Lion of Lucerne, but the deeds of valour which it recalls are not less notable, and both monuments commemorate that unbroken tradition of *Honneur et Fidelité* which has been the pride of the Swiss in foreign service.

Chapter XV

PILATUS AND BÜRGENSTOCK

1. Pilatus

PILATUS (6,995 ft.) probably owes its name to the fact that it is so often capped with cloud, for it is far more probable that the name is derived from the Latin word *pileatus* (capped) than from Pontius Pilate. Nevertheless, the mountain is bound up with the Pilate legend. Pontius Pilate, so the story runs, was condemned by the Emperor Tiberius, who decreed that he should be put to death in the most shameful possible manner. Hearing this, Pilate committed suicide. Tiberius concealed his chagrin, and philosophically remarked that a man whose own hand had not spared him had most certainly died the most shameful of deaths. Pilate's body was attached to a stone and flung into the Tiber, where it caused a succession of storms. The Romans decided to remove it, and the body was conveyed to Vienne as a mark of contempt for the people of that place. It was flung into the Rhone, and did its best to maintain its reputation. It was finally hurled into a little marshy lake near the summit of Pilatus. Here Pilate's behaviour was tolerable enough, though he resented indiscriminate stone-throwing into the lake by evoking terrible storms, and once a year he escaped from the waters and sat clothed in a scarlet robe on a rock near by. Anybody luckless enough to see him on these occasions died within the twelvemonth.

Access to the lake was forbidden to the citizens of Lucerne, and in 1307 six clerics were imprisoned for having

attempted an ascent without observing the local regula-
tions. Finally, in 1585, Pastor John Müller of Lucerne,
accompanied by a few courageous sceptics, visited the
lake, threw stones into the water, and shouted, " *Pilate,
wirf aus dein Kath.*" The taunts produced no effect, and
the legend received its final quietus.

Thirty years earlier Pilatus was ascended by one of the
most remarkable of the early mountaineers, Conrad Gesner,
a professor at Zürich, and the pioneer of mountaineering
literature. His mountaineering exploits were confined to
the lower hills, such as Pilatus. He had a genuine love
for the mountains, in an age when the mountains were
regarded with almost universal disgust, and he has left us
a charming description of his ascent of Pilatus. The
mountaineer, he tells us, is freed from the noisy tumult of
the city, and " in the profound, abiding silence one catches
echoes of the harmony of celestial spheres." There is
much more in the same key. He finds a simple joy in all
those simple things which make up a mountain walk.
The cool breezes playing on heated limbs, the sun's genial
warmth, the contrasts of outline, colour, and height, the
unending variety, so that " in one day you wander through
the four seasons of the year, spring, summer, autumn,
and winter."

Walkers can climb Pilatus from Hergiswil in four to
five hours but most people take the railway from
Alpnachstad, average gradient 38 : 100, maximum 48 : 100.
The view of the Bernese Alps is magnificent.

Alpnachstad, a station on the Brünig line, can be
reached by a lake steamer. Some steamers run direct to
Alpnachstad, but an alternative is to take the steamer
to Kehrsiten-Bürgenstock and then change on to one of
the steamers which run regularly from Weggis to
Alpnachstad via Kehrsiten-Bürgenstock.

The Alpnachersee is, in some ways, the most charming
part of the Lucerne Lake. As the steamer turns the

outlying spurs of Pilatus, the green plain beyond Alpnach, divided by the pointed spire of the church, is a perfect prelude to the Brünig hills, with the hint of the eternal snows beyond, the triple-crested Wetterhorn and the knife-edge which is the Eiger. The same steamer calls at Stansstad, the scene of a famous naval battle in 1315 (see page 40) and of a massacre during the French invasion (see page 100).

2. The Bürgenstock

Even the least observing of visitors to Lucerne can hardly escape a dim awareness of the Bürgenstock (2,996 ft.), for as night falls, the Hammetschwand Lift, 500 feet in height, sparkles into a vertical line of glittering lights.

The Bürgenstock group of hotels can be reached by car via Stansstad or by the lake steamers which touch at Kehrsiten whence the Bürgenstock hotels can be reached in ten minutes by cable railway. As you emerge from the top station you see the Eiger and Mönch beyond the Brünig hills. On the west side of the open space near the station you will see on an erratic boulder, deposited by ancient glaciers, a bronze bust of the founder of Bürgenstock, Franz Josef Bucher (1834–1906). Of the three Bürgenstock Hotels the oldest is the Grand Hotel, which was built in 1873. Your first walk will almost certainly be along the Felsenweg to the Hammetschwand Lift.

Just before you come to the Felsenweg you will pass on your right a charming little Gothic church, a modern copy of the little church of St. Jost on the Bürgenstock some little distance above Ennetburgen. St. Jost's (which should be visited) is the oldest church in Nidwalden.

The church on the Bürgenstock was built by Countess de la Baume, the daughter of a Belgian banker, by name Crombez, the elder of whose two sons was killed in the first world war and the second contracted consumption on active service from which he subsequently died. The church passed in 1922 into the possession of the present owner of the Bürgenstock hotels, Herr F. Frey-Fürst. The Gothic altar is probably the work of a carver from St. Gall. The Madonna is from Salzburg (*circa* 1450).

The Felsenweg, which is cut into the north face of the Bürgenstock, took five years to build. The Hammetschwand Lift is said to be the highest external lift in Europe. You can also continue along the Felsenweg and make the circuit of the mountain returning to the Bürgenstock by the Trogener Alp.

The Bürgenstock has, of course, tennis courts, and also an excellent golf links, but it has other things which are less easily matched elsewhere. My own most vivid memories of the Bürgenstock are of the sunsets which we watched as we dined in the Park Hotel. Our table was just beside the great window which faces north west. Below us was the lake where the evening steamers were weaving their fan-shaped patterns, the rippled water glinting like chain armour while the western sky slowly paled beyond the historic hills of Aargau. Due north we could see the bay of Küssnacht, and beyond it, a strip of blue haze which was the lake of Zug, and the sparkle of white houses storing up the last of the light. I never pass an ugly modern factory near Zug on my way to Zürich without a nostalgic sigh, for this factory stood out from the purple haze of evening, a conspicuous landmark from our Bürgenstock windows, a monolith of industrialism purged of much of its ugliness by the censorship of distance.

And I remember Bürgenstock for its varied patterns of enchanting walks, with easy gradients, many of them leading to the lake-side near Buochs or Stansstad— downhill walks adapted to the declining vigour of an ageing mountaineer, the return being made by cable railway. My favourite walk began with an easy half hour along the Buochs road to the saddle of Honegg which looks over the blue reaches of the eastern lake to the surge of rugged crests that hold the keys of the St. Gotthard. And from the Honegg an easy road leads to the steamer station of Ennetburgen, or you can prolong your walk to the charming little town of Buochs, whence you can return to Bürgenstock by steamer and cable railway. From Bürgenstock to Buochs you may reckon two hours or a brisk hour and a half.

A variant, which we enjoyed, was to turn sharp left near the Honegg past a hotel to the top of another lift which took us down to the lake shore whence we reached Weggis by a special motor boat service and returned to Bürgenstock by steamer and cable railway.

The Bürgenstock is not the only place with beautiful walks, and the dining room of the Park is not the only dining room overlooking a lovely lake, but there is one respect in which the Bürgenstock is unique. The group of hotels controlled by Herr F. Frey-Fürst combines two functions. They are hotels and they are also art galleries. There are of course other hotels which contain individual works of art of great beauty, the Palace at St. Moritz, for instance, where Herr Caspar Badrutt will show you, among other lovely things, a Raphael Madonna which he believes to be the original, the Dresden Madonna being, in his view, a copy. (Bad news this for the Russians who have removed Raphael's masterpiece to Moscow.) If there be hotels such as the Palace at St. Moritz which are enriched by works of art where is the precise justification for using the word "unique" in connection with the Bürgenstock? Because at the Bürgenstock you feel that the hotels would continue to exist as galleries even if the hotel aspect of them were as relatively unimportant as the luncheon room at the National Gallery. There are far more beautiful things on the Bürgenstock than in many art galleries. And where in the world can you find a hotel like the Palace at Bürgenstock, the lounge and library of which are adorned with Aubusson tapestries and Louis Quinze furniture, and the walls hung with Italian, Dutch and English masters, and the very bedrooms of which are hung with old prints, English and French.

Among the more important paintings in the Bürgenstock hotels are two Franz Snyders and a joint work by Snyders and Rubens at the Grand, a very characteristic landscape by Poussin, a fine portrait by William Deechey, and works by Dutch and German masters. The Palace has works by Winterhalter and Snyders, and a delightful painting by James Northcote.

The connoisseur of mountain art will find much to delight him at the Bürgenstock. My own guess is that the more naturalistic style of the past will once again come into fashion, and that Alexandre Calame (1810–1864), who has kept a small but convinced circle of admirers through all changes of fashion, will come into his own again. He has never painted anything finer than Mont Blanc from Chamonix, a work which he completed in 1846, and which hangs in the Grand Park Hotel. Calame is also represented by one of his own favourite themes, Rosenlaui, and also a study of the Tosender mountain torrent. In the same hotel there is a painting of the Oeschinensee by his promising pupil, Gustav Castan, and a painting of the waterfall above Brienz by his teacher, the Genevese painter François Diday.

If I had never met Herr F. Frey-Fürst, I might have pictured a sensitive aesthete who had lost his way and strayed into the hotel business, but I soon learned that the patience and discernment which he has displayed in making his famous collection was equalled by the patience and skill which he has shown in collecting from the different peasants the necessary plots of land to build his golf course. One peasant proved particularly obdurate. He accepted everything that Herr Frey-Fürst gave him including a free pass on the cable railway but relapsed into taciturnity when asked to state a price. Like Bacon he was " bribable but incorruptible " and then, one day, when Herr Frey-Fürst was calling on the peasant he disclosed the secret of his opposition in a casual but contemptuous allusion to " you city people." " But why do you call me a city person? " asked Herr Frey-Fürst. " I am the son of a peasant, just as you are." " Prove it," said the peasant. " Here is a cow. Milk her." Whereupon Herr Frey-Fürst took off his coat, sat down on the milking-stool and milked the cow to his own, to the peasant's and presumably to the cow's complete satisfaction. " You can have the land," said the peasant, " and I will let you have it for less than you offered."

Chapter XVI

THE RIGI AND THE RIGI RIVIERA

THE Rigi Riviera extends from the promontory of Hertenstein to Brunnen along the southern base of the Rigi. It is sheltered from the northern winds and exposed to the south.

Hertenstein, Weggis, Vitznau and Gersau are all popular holiday centres, and I have particularly happy memories of Weggis and Hertenstein.

Weggis comes back to me in a blaze of remembered colour, the pink chestnuts, the copper beeches, the lilac, gelder roses, and the tender green of beech trees. I remember orange blossom in the shady garden of the Hotel Albana which stoops to the lake, and the soft and southern tenderness of the sunsets which we could see from our veranda, and Pilatus, a confusion of golden and purple tones, as the western sky fought its rearguard battles with the night. Weggis, in general, and the Albana Hotel in particular, have something which will always bring me back.

Weggis and the Rigi Riviera can be reached either by road or by the lake. Let us begin by describing the road route.

1. Weggis, Vitznau and Gersau

Shortly after leaving Lucerne we pass the tram terminus of Halde where you will notice the lower station of the cable railway which leads in eight minutes to the Dietschiberg, often called the Little Rigi. There is a fine golf course near the summit, which incidentally can easily be reached by car, and a charming view of the lake and the distant Oberland. I remember sitting in the Dietschiberg restaurant watching a hawk hover over the Lake of

Lucerne. The " Little Rigi " contains among many other attractions a superb model railway. This is the work of a brilliant engineer whose family bitterly regret that he gave up his profession in order to build the world's finest model railway. We had some talk with him. He described with a gleam in his eye some branch line which he was proposing to open. He drew our attention to the miniature tunnel and the perfect reproduction of a restaurant car. This brilliant young man will never grow rich on the tickets which he sells to those who want to see his railway, but I can also see his point. It is much easier to become a rich and successful engineer than to enter the select class of those who have produced something which is absolutely the best of its kind, even if that kind be nothing more than a model railway.

Before you reach Küssnacht you should stop and visit the little chapel built by King Leopold of the Belgians in memory of his wife, Queen Astrid, who was killed in a motoring accident just opposite the chapel. At Küssnacht the road to the Lake of Zug turns sharply to the left, and the road to the Rigi Riviera sharp right. The road to Immensee on Lake Zug passes the church and ascends to the right to the Hohle Gasse at the upper end of which is Tell's chapel, built in 1522 and restored in 1895, marking the spot where Gessler is said to have been shot by Tell. The chapel, which must not be confused with the other Tell's chapel near Brunnen, was probably built on the site of an earlier chapel (see page 34).

The road to Weggis follows the Küssnacht bay to Greppen and reaches the lake again between Hertenstein and Weggis and thence follows the Riviera past Vitznau and Gersau to Brunnen (24 miles from Lucerne).

If you are stopping at Weggis ask the concierge for the local map on which a series of delightful walks are marked. You can, for instance, reach Hertenstein either by the main road, or by a lovely walk along unfrequented paths.

L

The Rigi railway was originally planned to start from Weggis, but the muleteers who were doing well out of providing mules for tourists to the Rigi summit raised such a riot that the plans were changed to the detriment of Weggis and certainly not to the benefit of the muleteers, for the railway was built in spite of their opposition, and all that they achieved was to ensure that the railway started from Weggis' rival, Vitznau.

The motor road to Brunnen passes two popular lake centres, Vitznau and Gersau. Gersau for five hundred years was the smallest sovereign State of Europe, three miles by two in area, containing less than two thousand inhabitants. Gersau was originally bought by the Habsburgs from two of its richest inhabitants. The villagers saved up their pence, and in the course of time bought their own village from the mortgage-holders. The relations between Gersau and Lucerne were often strained. Lucerne laid claim to the little State, but the liberties of this tiny republic were reaffirmed by the Emperor Sigismund in 1433. In the course of these disputes the Lucernois carried out a nocturnal raid on Gersau, and hung a man of straw on the gallows as a token of their contempt for the claims of Gersau to jurisdiction over life and limb. The men of Gersau replied by decking the dummy in the colours of Lucerne. This effective retort enraged Lucerne, and would have led to bloodshed had not the Confederates imposed a compromise. The men of Gersau were told to remove the colours of Lucerne, and the men of Lucerne had to remove the corpse.

Gersau was incorporated in the Helvetic Republic by Napoleon, but re-emerged as a sovereign State in 1814, and dispatched an expeditionary force of no less than 24 men to join the allied armies on the return of Napoleon from Elba. The victorious allies proved grossly ungrateful for these reinforcements, and incorporated Gersau with Schwyz in 1818.

2. The Rigi

What are the seven best views in the Alps? My own list is as follows. The Oberland from the Faulhorn, the Matterhorn from the Riffelalp, the Mont Blanc range from the Brévent, the Valaisan Alps and Mont Blanc from Montana, the view from the Rigi, the distant view of the Alps from the Weissenstein and the view from the terraces of San Remigio above Pallanza.

I am sure that the Rigi (5,905 ft.) would be on the first seven list of all those who know the Alps from end to end. It is a panorama which includes, as three of my first seven views do not include, lakes as well as mountains, the Küssnacht bay of the Lake of Lucerne and the Zugersee at our feet, the Lowerz lake in the middle distance, a glimpse of the Lake of Zürich, and in the distance, historic Sempach, Baldegger and Hallwiler lakes. The mountain panorama extends from the Säntis past the Tödi and Titlis to the Bernese Oberland.

The Rigi is composed of conglomerate and molasse sandstone. It is formed from the remains of old torrent beds. The Rigi is the southern slope of the great arch of Miocene pudding-stone, and the summit and most of the northern slope has disappeared. The gravel beds formed beneath the torrents which swept down from long-vanished mountains provided the material from which the Rigi was built. Conglomerate is one of the few forms of rock which really suggests its origin to the uninitiated. It requires an act of faith to believe that the limestone ranges of the Alps were built up, inch by inch, by slow deposits of limestone underneath the vast ocean which covered that which is now Switzerland, but the great gravel beds which form the Rigi, with rounded boulders and pebbles wedged into the coarser sandstone, suggest even to the layman a vivid picture of an earlier age.

Towards the end of the seventeenth century a pious Catholic, Sebastian Zay by name, who was distressed by the fact that the herdsmen on the Rigi had so few opportunities for hearing Mass, built a little chapel on the north slopes of the Rigi at a place which was called Klösterli (4,320 ft.), and which is now a station on the line from Arth-Goldau. This chapel, built in 1688, was served by Capuchins. It was rebuilt in 1715. It is still visited by many pilgrims on July 2nd and September 8th. Before the end of the seventeenth century there were no less than three small inns near the chapel. A Zürich professor, Leonhard Meister, who climbed the Rigi in 1781, tells us that as many as 14,000 pilgrims used to take part in the September pilgrimage to the Klösterli chapel.

The first inn on the summit of the Rigi was opened in August 1816, and the first names in the Visitors' Book are those of three Englishmen, W. Haggit, Sir Henry Lambert and Colonel Lambert.

In 1820 William Wordsworth and his sister Dorothy paid a prolonged visit to Lake Lucerne. Wordsworth wrote a series of sonnets inspired by the historic background of the lake. None of these are of great interest, for it was the English lakeland mountains which inspired Wordsworth's best mountain poetry, his sonnet on the Simplon being the only Alpine poem in which his authentic genius found expression. As a word painter of Alpine scenery he is inferior to his brilliant sister Dorothy. Here is her description of the view from the Rigi:

Meanwhile, we were assailed by ruffling breezes and gusty rain-drops—yet I cannot express the quietness of the valley sounds of matin bells, alike descending to our ears through dense or light vapours—or in their partial clearing away, when houses and churches were descried, how far below! The rain was over before the sun was above the mountain line of our horizon. A part of the orb appeared below a canopy of rosy clouds into which it passed in the moment of ascent. Some of the distant Pikes were touched by glowing hues; but only touched; and the hues were gone.

And here by way of contrast is a famous passage in Mark Twain's *A Tramp Abroad*.

Mark Twain and Harris had walked up the Rigi and were so exhausted that they slept right through till sunset. They were aroused by the alpine horn and wrapping themselves in blankets rushed out to the scaffolding on the peak of the summit.

Presently Harris exclaimed—" Why, —nation, it's going down! "

Perfectly true. We had missed the *morning* horn-blow, and slept all day. This was stupefying. Harris said:—

" Look here, the sun isn't the spectacle—it's *us*—stacked up here on top of this gallows, in these idiotic blankets, and two hundred and fifty well-dressed men and women down there gawking up at us and not caring a straw whether the sun rises or sets, as long as they've got such a ridiculous spectacle as this to set down in their memorandum-books. They seem to be laughing their ribs loose, and there's one girl there that appears to be going all to pieces. I never saw such a man as you before. I think you are the very last possibility in the way of an ass."

" What have I done? " I answered with heat.

" What have you done? You've got up at half-past seven o'clock in the evening to see the sun rise, that's what you've done."

" And have you done any better, I'd like to know? I always used to get up with the lark, till I came under the petrifying influence of your turgid intellect."

" You used to get up with the lark! Oh, no doubt; you'll get up with the hangman one of these days."

Many years later in a letter to Twichell, the " Harris " of *A Tramp Abroad*, Mark Twain wrote:—

O Switzerland! The further it recedes into the enriching haze of time, the more intolerably delicious the charm of it and the sheer joy of it and the glory and majesty and solemnity and pathos of it grow. . . . There are mountains and mountains and mountains in this world, but only these take you by the heartstrings. I wonder what the secret of it is. Well, time and again it has seemed to me that I must drop everything and flee to Switzerland once more. It is a *longing*—a deep, strong, tugging longing—that is the word. We must go again, Joe.

Many Rigi enthusiasts stay for weeks at Rigi Kaltbad or Rigi-First. There are many lovely walks—walks which involve very little climbing—on the plateau of the Rigi. One of the most beautiful walks in the Alps leads from the Kaltbad to the Rigi Scheidegg four miles away, and about 500 feet higher than the Kaltbad.

Chapter XVII

BRUNNEN

BRUNNEN is an important station on the Gotthard line. It can be reached by train from Lucerne, by steamer, or by one or other of two beautiful roads—the road which branches off at Küssnacht and follows the north shore of the Rigi Riviera or the road which leads from Küssnacht through Arth and Schwyz. The distance is approximately the same whichever road you take, twenty-four miles from Lucerne to Brunnen.

Brunnen is the birthplace of the Swiss confederation and lies almost opposite Rütli, " the immortal meadow " (see pp. 22 to 36). The steamer which transports you from Brunnen to the landing stage for the Rütli meadow passes a curious pointed rock sticking out of the lake and adorned with Schiller's name.

1. Schiller's William Tell

Friedrich Schiller was born on November 10th, 1759, in the Duchy of Wurtemberg. He was the son of a lieutenant in the Wurtemberg Army. As a boy he wanted to take Orders but he was forcibly removed from the " Latin School," which candidates for Orders attended, and transferred on the instructions of the all-powerful Duke of Wurtemberg to another school where the secular curriculum would make it impossible for him to become a clergyman. In 1780 he was posted as a doctor to the Auge regiment in Stuttgart.

Schiller was an exceptionally fortunate man. His mediocre plays and poetry happened to coincide with the mental fashion of the moment, and whereas geniuses have starved and writers of outstanding talent have failed to find publishers for their writings, or producers for their plays, this young army doctor had no sooner written *Die Raüber* than it was accepted by the director of the Mannheim National Theatre, and in due course performed. Even more amazing than his success in foisting his indifferent plays on the public was his career as a historian. His book on the history of the Rebellion in the Netherlands was an immediate success. It is perhaps not surprising that this book appealed to the public, for Schiller was the first German populariser of history, a German H. G. Wells with the same cheerful capacity for subordinating fact to ideology, but what is astonishing is that he should, on the basis of this unscholarly work, have been appointed to the Chair of History at Jena. This is much as if H. G. Wells had been appointed Regius Professor of History at Oxford. A recent and friendly biographer, Professor H. G. Garland, comments on " his bold sweeping statements which neglect fact and detail . . . he lived as a historian from hand to mouth. He did not know enough facts and he did not know the relative value of his sources," but Professor Garland adds benignly that Schiller " had profited by a visit to the world of facts, even if he found its climate uncongenial." How uncongenial is apparent in most of his plays. We do not go to a dramatist for exact history, to Homer, for instance, for a description of the Siege of Troy which would provide material for a lecture at a Staff College, but even poets and dramatists have to confine their fancy within a loose framework of accepted fact or, at least, of accepted tradition, if they hope to carry conviction. A modern dramatist who represented the Greeks raising the Siege of Troy, and Hector leading a counter invasion of Greece would not escape as lightly as Schiller who, with his usual luck, got away with a travesty of the facts about St. Joan. Schiller's St. Joan falls in love with an English knight, is denounced by her father as a witch, is captured by the English, delivered by a miracle, and dies fighting gloriously on the battlefield.

In his most popular play, *William Tell*, he mugged up a few facts and took his local colour from travel books. He himself had never visited Switzerland, but then Shakespeare probably never saw Verona, and it is highly improbable that Homer ever saw Troy. And the play might still be a great play, in spite of anachronisms such as making a character talk about " Switzerland " long before there was such a place, or absurdities such as chamois hunters cutting their feet in order to adhere to the rocks by their blood, a technique which the Alpine Club has yet to rediscover. And it would perhaps be hypercritical to insist that the play is unhistorical, not only in detail, but in its attempt to reconstruct the social climate of the Forest Cantons.

The *Iliad* is no doubt as remote from the real facts of the Trojan War as Schiller's *William Tell* from the realities of the Forest Cantons under the Habsburgs, but whereas Schiller's play is hopelessly dated, the *Iliad* lives because its noblest lines have a timeless quality. Great lines in poetry have this timeless quality and that is why, as Newman said, lines which are " the birth of some chance morning or evening at an Ionian festival among the Sabine hills " come home to the reader " when he has experience of life and pierce him with their sad earnestness and vivid exactness." There are some well-known Schiller tags, and some competent poems which appeal to his admirers, but he never wrote a single line which has a timeless and a universal appeal.

I remember watching the rose of sunset fade from the Oberland snows when the Germans were breaking through the gap near ill-fated Sedan, and wondering whether the Swastika would be flying from the roofs of Berne if and when I returned to Switzerland, and the words of Hector to his wife came back to me, his words before he left her for his last fight:—

" May I be dead and the earth cover me before I know thee to be a slave."

I doubt if any line of Schiller's has ever come back with equal force at a great crisis of fear and sorrow.

Schiller was a successful dramatist because he proclaimed a gospel which was already wholeheartedly accepted by those to whom his gospel was addressed. The fact that none of his characters come alive did not matter because he was writing for people far more interested in noble sentiments than in interesting personalities. His work appealed to the ideologists who, as Burke somewhere remarks, were so preoccupied with the rights of man that they had totally forgotten his nature. Schiller was writing for " Dawnists " who believed that the dark night of tyranny was nearly over and the dawn of freedom and justice very near. " How beautiful, O Man," exclaimed Schiller, " you stand in the closing years of the century, the palm of victory in your hand, proud, noble, manly."

I am sure that Schiller's Posa brought down the house when he described himself as *Ein Abgeorneter der ganzen Menschheit* (a representative of all Humanity) for the Humanity-Mongers were at the beginning of their career and the shape of Humanitarianism to come was still unpredicted. Schiller, to do him justice, was profoundly shocked a few years later by the actual performances of that great " representative of Humanity," Robespierre.

What Hazlitt said of Shelley is equally true of Schiller. " He was clogged by no dull system of reality, no earthbound feelings, no rooted prejudices, by nothing that belongs to the mighty trunk and hard husk of nature, but is drawn up by irresistible levity to the region of bare speculative fancy."

Schiller's personal character was attractive. He was a good and affectionate husband and he put up a stout fight against the illness which killed him at the age of forty-five (May 9th, 1805).

I have described him as lucky, but his financial rewards were always small in comparison with his prestige. In Schiller's Germany, copyright could only be secured as a privilege from a reigning prince and this was restricted to the particular German principality for which it was granted.

The Mythenstein is a rock which rises about eighty feet from the surface of the lake, and on this rock, which Nature provided free, you can read in gilded letters that the Forest Cantons desire to record their gratitude to Schiller. Inexpensive gratitude, but an adequate, even if unconsciously adequate, tribute to a very indifferent play.

2. Shelley at Brunnen

On July 28th, 1814, Shelley left England with Mary Godwin and Mary's stepsister, Jane Clairemont, usually known as Claire, a name which she adopted and imposed on her family and her friends. They drove to Paris and decided to walk from Paris to Switzerland through a country with which Britain had been at war for twenty years, and which was then overrun with a recently demobilised army after a demoralising defeat. Shelley bought an ass to carry the luggage, but the ass revolted and was disposed of at Charenton where they bought a mule for ten Napoleons. "About nine o'clock," writes Mary, "we departed. We were clad in black silk. I rode on the mule which carried also our portmanteau, Shelley and Claire followed."

From Troyes Shelley wrote a letter to the wife he had left in England. Fearing lest she might misinterpret his elopement as indicating some light diminution in his loyalty and in his affection, he hastened to assure her of the constancy of his devotion.

I write to show you that I do not forget you; I write to urge you to come to Switzerland, where you will at least find one firm and constant friend, to whom your interests will always be dear—by whom your feelings will never be wilfully injured. From none can you expect this but me—all others are either unfeeling or selfish, or have beloved friends of their own.

The fascinating thing about this letter is its shattering sincerity. Shelley was as incapable of doing anything which he believed to be wrong as of making the least attempt to conform to what the world believed right. There is something inhuman about Shelley, a suggestion of an Elemental incarnate in human form, a refugee from a realm in which the Ten Commandments are not valid. Mr. Sydney Scott's Trilogy of hitherto unpublished letters (*The Athenians, Harriet and Mary, Shelley at Oxford*, The Golden Cockerel Press) confirms me in my belief that Shelley was not wholly sane. He had the serene untroubled conscience of a small child even when he was behaving most outrageously. Surely there is a touch of genuine insanity in the letter which he wrote to the wife he was deserting and in his enthusiastic invitation to his friend, Jefferson Hogg, to take full advantage of Mary Shelley's affectionate advances, for the sentence quoted from Shelley's letter to Hogg on page 51 of *Harriet and Mary* is difficult to explain in any other sense. And no sane man could, in the same letter, write: " Let this horrid Galilean rule the canaille then," and " I took the Sacrament with her on Sunday." " Shelley," writes Ethel Colburn Mayne, " is pinnacled almost alone in his seraphic gravity. Byron, on the contrary, touched humanity at every point." " Shelley," wrote Byron to Murray on August 3rd, 1822, " was without exception the best and least selfish man I ever knew." And to Lady Blessington he described him as, " full of delicacy, disinterested beyond all other men. . . . He had formed to himself a beau ideal of all that is fine, high minded, and noble, and he acted up to this ideal even to the very letter." He did indeed, even when he was running away from his wife.

The mule that had been bought in exchange for the ass was sold at Troyes and replaced by an open voiture, and three weeks after landing at Calais, Shelley, Mary and Claire crossed the Swiss frontier near Pontarlier. Shelley had just turned twenty-two and Mary was within a few weeks of her seventeenth birthday. They travelled via St. Sulpice and Neuchâtel, near which they had their first view of the High Alps, to Lucerne, whence they went by boat to Brunnen.

Mary Shelley, a gifted writer, and the authoress of a best-seller, *Frankenstein*, has left us a description of their first day at Brunnen.

Brunnen is situated on the northern side of the angle which the lake makes, forming the extremity of the lake of Lucerne. Here we rested for the night, and dismissed our boatmen. Nothing could be more magnificent than the view from this spot. The high mountains encompassed us, darkening the waters; at a distance on the shores of Uri, we could perceive the chapel of Tell, and this was the village where he matured the conspiracy which was to overthrow the tyrant of his country; and, indeed, this lovely lake, these sublime mountains, and wild forests, seemed a fit cradle for a mind aspiring to high adventure and heroic deeds. Yet we saw no glimpse of his spirit in his present countrymen. The Swiss appeared to us then, and experience has confirmed our opinion, a people slow of comprehension and of action; but habit has made them unfit for slavery, and they would, I have little doubt, make a brave defence against any invader of their freedom.

Such were our reflections, and we remained until late in the evening on the shores of the lake, conversing, enjoying the rising breeze, and contemplating with feelings of exquisite delight the divine objects that surrounded us.

The following day was spent on a consideration of our circumstances, and in contemplation of the scene around us. A furious *vent d'Italie* (South wind) tore up the lake, making immense waves, and carrying the water in a whirlwind high in the air, when it fell like heavy rain into the lake. The waves broke with a tremendous noise on the rocky shores. This conflict continued during the whole day, but it became calmer towards the evening. S . . . and I walked on the banks, and sitting on a rude pier, S . . . read aloud the account of the Siege of Jerusalem from Tacitus.

They did not stay long in Brunnen. It had cost them £60 to cross France, and the discovery that they had only £28 left compelled them to return home as quickly as possible and by the cheapest possible route. They cut things pretty fine, but fortunately Shelley's wife Harriet was able to pay the cab which delivered Shelley at her door.

I tried while I was at Brunnen to discover whether the house in which the Shelleys stayed could be traced.

" It would be rather nice," I said to Herr Williman of the Grand Hotel, Brunnen, a few days after the pound had been devalued to twelve francs, " to put a tablet on the place he stayed in if we could find it. He had to leave in a great hurry because he ran out of money."

" That is very *actuel*," said Herr Williman thoughtfully. " If you can't find the place, why not put the tablet on the wall of this hotel? "

Herr Williman married the daughter of Herr Benziger who built the Grand Hotel, and who became the most famous portrait painter in America and the founder of the well-known Catholic publishing firm which bears his name. His paintings give distinction to the Grand Hotel.

3. Days at Brunnen

A coloured photograph of the Bay of Uri hung in our dining-room at home, and was one of the first mountain views to imprint its clear outlines on my mind as a child. How secure was that Victorian world in which that photograph had been taken! How little of that world remains! But the Uri-Rothstock remains, and the gentle curve of its crest is unchanged. There is something faintly irritating about the immutability of the mountains, and their serene indifference to the "troubles of our proud and angry dust." The Uri-Rothstock would look no less benign if Rütli, the birthplace of Swiss freedom, were to be desecrated by a statue of Stalin, the Liberator.

But perhaps it would be more reasonable to give thanks that there is a beauty which even man cannot mar. Certainly the glory of this panorama from the balcony at the Grand Hotel tempts me to find a new application for Balzac's remark that a Frenchman need not travel because he can find within the frontiers of France everything which a sane man would wish to see. Why travel in search of views when one can spend the day watching the changing tone and texture of this supremely lovely lake? And what mountainscape could be more perfectly composed than this? The central mass of the Seelisberg is the unifying focus of a great design. The gentle rise of the separate and successive western ridges to the crest of the Seelisberg provides the perfect foil to the sharp plunge into the lake of the cliffs which stoop from the eastern shoulders of the Seelisberg into the Bay of Uri.

The rhythm of this view, the suggestion of ridge echoing ridge has a curiously operatic effect. No wonder that Wagner wanted to build a chalet at Brunnen, or that King Ludwig of Bavaria found it difficult to leave. The King stayed on for week after week, as the guest of Herr Benziger, father of the painter, and when the moon was full he used to leave the Benziger villa and row across the bay to Rütli and awaken with a Wagnerian horn reverberating echoes in the moonlit cliffs.

4. Expeditions from Brunnen

Brunnen is a perfect base for expeditions. Schwyz and Einsiedeln are within easy reach. And so is Morgarten. You can spend half a day in Lucerne, Zug, Engelberg or Andermatt and return the same evening to Brunnen, and Brunnen is one of the best places on the lake for the most famous motor tour in the Alps—the tour of the three passes described below.

A pleasant saunter which will give an idea of the lie of the land is to begin at the steamer quay, and then walk along the lake front to the west, past the Waldstätterhof, a hotel of many happy memories, and then turn sharply to the right along a charming little canal, faintly reminiscent of Bruges. Cross the street, walk through the pretty grounds of the Park Hotel which is linked with the famous Hellerbad Electric Baths, for which well-substantiated claims have been made, and where the cure lasts ten days instead of the three weeks normal at other establishments. Follow the path beyond the hotel which finally brings you out into the main street. On your way back to the lakeside you pass a little chapel which was built by a member of the von Reding family in 1620 after the old chapel had been burnt in the fire which destroyed so many buildings in Brunnen.

A rack-and-pinion railway leads from Brunnen (1,443 ft.) to Morschach (2,116 ft.) and thence to Axenstein (2,323 ft.) which commands a magnificent view over the two arms of Lake Lucerne, a view which was highly praised by Queen Victoria and—which is rather more to the point—by the great painter, Calame. The Anglican chapel near the hotel recalls the Victorian age when Axenstein was full of English visitors from the middle of June onwards. Even in the 1921 Baedeker there is a laconic statement eloquent in its evidence of change: " English Church (All Saints; no services in 1921)."

You can walk down from Morschach by a pleasant path

THE BÜRGENSTOCK

THE URI-ROTHSTOCK
from Axenstein above Brunnen

through beech trees with blue glimpses of the lake below,
or you can descend from Axenstein by a path which turns
sharply to the right after emerging from the station.
About twenty minutes from the hotel you pass, on the left,
a boulder about 25 feet high which is the only example
that I have yet discovered in the Alps of a boulder which
is absolutely inaccessible without artificial aids such as
pitons. Every other boulder that I have seen has had
some weak point in its defence.

You can cross the lake to Beckenried and take the
Klewenalp cable railway, very popular with skiers in
winter, but inferior as a view point to the Rigi or Pilatus.
You can reach Stoos (4,265 ft.) either by a two hours' walk
from Morschach, or by tram, road and funicular from
Schwyz, and from Stoos you can take a chair-lift to near
the summit of the Frohnalpstock (6,306 ft.). In winter
Stoos is also very popular with skiers.

Obviously you will visit Rütli, and you will be unwise not
to devote a day to the Seelisberg. The steamer station is
Treib, where the charming old inn was rebuilt in 1903.
Thence by cable railway to Seelisberg (2,635 ft.). The
pilgrimage chapel of Maria-Sonnenberg has some entertaining *ex votos*. We particularly liked the *ex voto* con-
tributed by a top-hatted gentleman from Cincinatti, but
the *ex voto* which was really *actuel* was apparently offered in
thanksgiving for the timely arrival of a cook. From this
chapel an easy downhill walk leads past the little Seelisberg
lake to Rütli.

From the steamer station at Isleten, near the east end of
the lake, a motor bus takes you up the Isental. From the
village of that name the Uri-Rothstock (9,615 ft.) may be
climbed without difficulty.

Brunnen is one of the best centres on the lake for the
finest full day's motoring in the Alps, the tour of three
passes, Susten, Grimsel and Furka. This circular tour
begins and ends at Wassen between Flüelen and Göschenen,

M

and therefore the nearer your base to Wassen the better. The round tour from and back to Wassen across the three passes totals about 83 miles, and involves an aggregate ascent of 10,256 feet. Wassen is 24 miles from Brunnen, so the round trip from Brunnen involves 107 miles of motoring and an aggregate ascent of nearly 13,000 feet. (For mileage details see appendix.)

The Susten road which was completed during the second world war is, perhaps, the most perfectly engineered mountain motor road in the world. The cost was thirty-one million francs. The Three-Passes tour (Susten–Grimsel–Furka) is, I think, best done beginning with the Susten from Wassen, for the views of the Wetterhörner are best seen on the descent from the Susten to Innertkirchen, and the Grimsel route is finest when taken from Meiringen. Look out for the artificial lake at the Grimsel with the magnificent view of the Finsteraarhorn. From the summit of the Furka on clear days you can see the Matterhorn and Weisshorn.

Chapter XVIII

"THE UNBOUGHT GRACE OF LIFE"

1. The Ital Reding House

THERE is perhaps no Canton in which the Swiss bourgeoise art of the Renaissance and Baroque can be studied to greater advantage than in Schwyz. Schwyz, the matrix of Switzerland, is a small Canton, and its capital is a " dorf " rather than a metropolis. No Schwyzois would allow you to describe it as a " Stadt," but in Schwyz you realise that importance is not measured by the physical scale of magnitude. It was in this little " dorf," under the shadow of the Mythen, that Switzerland was born, and it was from the patrician houses in and near this miniature capital that many of the regimental commanders came who made the Swiss regiments famous in Europe. There is something aloof and self-sufficient in the autarchic appearance of these great houses, such as the Grosshaus (1604), the seat of the Papal Nunciature in the early nineteenth century. It is indeed Swiss patrician homes such as these that Henry James described in his story, *At Isella*. He writes:—

I wondered of course who lived in them, and how they lived and what was society in Altdorf, longing plaintively, in the manner of roaming Americans, for a few stray crumbs from the native social board, with my fancy vainly beating its wings against the great blank wall, behind which, in travel-haunted Europe, all gentle private interests nestle away from intrusion. Here, as elsewhere, I was struck with the mere surface-relation of the Western tourist to the soil he treads. He filters and trickles through the dense social body in every possible direction, and issues forth at last the same virginal waterdrop. " Go your way," these antique houses seemed to say, from their quiet courts and gardens, " the road is yours and welcome, but the land is ours. You may pause and stare and wonder, but you may never know us! "

Perhaps the most famous of these patrician homes is the Ital Reding Haus, not very far from the church, which dates from the beginning of the seventeenth century. The family of von Reding has its roots in Swiss history. The von Redings maintained the great military tradition of the family by raising regiments in the service of the Kings of France, of Spain and of Naples. A von Reding fought - under Pfyffer during the famous retreat from Meaux. You will find the name of von Reding on the Lion memorial at Lucerne, for a von Reding died with the Swiss Guard. It was the von Reding commemorated by Wordsworth who commanded the last desperate defence of the Schwyzois in their resistance to the French revolutionary armies. In the Peninsular War the French general Dupont was trapped at Baylen, and routed by a Spanish army under " a Swiss Commander with the unlikely name of Reding," to quote from Philip Guedalla's generally admirable biography of Wellington, which is very much as if one wrote that England was saved in 1940 by a Prime Minister " with the unlikely name of Churchill."

The Ital Reding Haus contains many lovely things, some fascinating pieces of seventeenth- and eighteenth-century furniture, a charming Oriel window, a good Renaissance painting on the ceiling, a Venetian chandelier, some good family portraits and a fine specimen of a floor of inlaid wood. Even more evocative of what Burke calls " the unbought grace of life " was the gracious lady who received us. How can I describe Frau von Reding? Medium height, slim, grey hair . . . those are the details which might be mentioned on a passport, but no passport would mention the soft modulations of her voice or the beauty which had defied the siege of time. She wore a jabot trimmed with beautiful old lace on a soft blue frock. Though she carried her years well there was something about her which suggested a *revenant* from the eighteenth century—as if she had been brought up at the Court of Versailles. She spoke of the French Revolution as if it had been quite a recent outrage. "The canaille butchered my great, great uncle in the Tuileries. France has never recovered and will never recover from the revolution." She showed us an old print of Paris in the mid-eighteenth century. A little group waiting for their Sedan chairs after Mass, ladies with powdered hair and courtly nobles. "Life was very lovely then," said Frau von Reding, as if like Talleyrand she was sighing for "*la douceur de la vie avant* 1789."

The contrast between this gentle lady and the warlike climate of her home was curiously impressive. Her walls were hung with prints of old battles. The seventeenth-century stove was adorned with representations of Morgarten, Sempach and Grandson. Even the inlaid floor with its Turks' heads recalled the days when a von Reding had commanded a regiment against the Turks. The walls were hung with portraits of the fighting von Redings. The type has persisted from century to century with its strong aquiline nose and keen intelligent eyes. "The von Redings," said their descendant, "did not know the meaning of fear" and I knew that she regretted that the von Redings of to-day have been denied the chance to prove their mettle under fire, and have indeed had less experience of the peril of war than millions of women in the belligerent countries, such as the lady to whom this remark was addressed, women who know from personal experience whether they can or cannot stand up to bombs.

It really was a pity [sighed Frau von Reding] that the Swiss regiments in foreign service were disbanded. There was a time when Switzerland had the most powerful army on the continent. In the fifteenth century the Swiss soldier was without rival, and since then the von Reding regiment and others kept alive our great military tradition, but the Radicals hated this tradition. They cannot bear anything with tradition behind it. Ah those Radicals! *Sie sind unverbesserlich* [they are incorrigible].

During the last war we celebrated the hundred and fiftieth anniversary of the massacre of the Swiss guards by a ceremony at the Löwen Denkmal [Lion Memorial] in Lucerne. Colonel Pfyffer organised it. Some of the descendants of the old families who had served the king of France turned up in the old uniforms, and answered *Hier* when the roll-call of the dead officers was called and there was a Mass for the repose of their souls. But the Bundesrat was not represented. They were frightened of the Radicals. And General Guisan did not come. . . .

The old Switzerland is disappearing. My husband did not like the State. The State, he said, is a tyrant. It is the duty of the State to spend as little money as possible and to interfere as little as possible. But those ideas are no longer fashionable. . . . Still here in Schwyz we still do what we can to defend our freedom.

We left her with regret and we returned from the eighteenth to the twentieth century. I was worried by an elusive memory. Something I had read reminded me of Frau von Reding. . . . Ah yes, of course . . . Frau von Reding recalled the passage in which Dorothy Wordsworth describes the great lady whom she saw in Schwyz:

A tall grave middle-aged woman had entered. . . . I found her seated, and could not but fix my eyes on her the moment I entered the room. A company of peasants of inferior rank were at supper at one end, we at our tea-table in a distant corner, and she, at a third table, ate her supper alone, being served with ceremony like a person of distinction. Not one of us, I am sure, can ever forget this gentlewoman (for such I must call her). The involuntary notice she drew from us did not seem absolutely to offend—yet I cannot say she was pleased with it. She seemed to be an adequate representative of the Helvetian Matronage, as the Mother of the Gracchi might have been of the Roman, and some of our party were reminded, by her appearance and deportment, of the complaint made by the French, that, while stationed in this country, they could neither procure a mistress nor a spy.

2. Schwyz, Town and Canton

The town of Schwyz was burnt down in 1642, and the parish church, built in 1643, was pulled down and rebuilt in 1770 by Jakob and Johann Singer. The late rococo stalls of the choir are very entertaining. The best thing in the Ratsaal which was restored in 1891 is the little room which was built in 1649.

An excellent guide to the town can be obtained locally, *Schwyz* by Dr. Anton Cassell, and specialists should consult (if they can secure or borrow a copy) Dr. Birchler's classic *Kunstdenkmäler des Kantons Schwyz*. The historic pass of Morgarten may be visited on the way to the Abbey of Einsiedeln.

The motorist who visits Brunnen from Lucerne should, as I have elsewhere suggested, drive to Brunnen by the Rigi Riviera and return by the shores of the Lowerzersee and Zugersee, and in this case, he should make the slight detour involved by visiting the town of Schwyz.

The road from Schwyz joins the road from Brunnen at Seewen, whence we drive along the southern shore of the lovely Lowerz Lake to Arth-Goldau, which is connected with the summit of the Rigi by railway. The station is situated on the scene of the terrible Goldau landslide, mentioned by Byron, which fell from the slopes of the Rossberg in 1806. The Rossberg consists of beds of sandstone and conglomerate resting on soft argillaceous layers. The upper strata were soaked by the heavy rains of the winter of 1806, and suddenly slid off the underlying beds, and swept down across the valley. Goldau and three other villages were buried in the *débris*. Part of the Lake of Lowerz was filled up, and more than four hundred and fifty people were killed in this catastrophe. The scar on the Rossberg from which this avalanche descended is still clearly visible.

There is a fine baroque church at Arth on the Zuger-see, the south shore of which is followed to Immensee where we turn sharply to the left and join the route, described in Chapter XVI, at Küssnacht.

Chapter XIX

ZUG

1. Early History

ZUG is on the line between Lucerne and Zürich but few indeed are the tourists who break their journey at Zug, and yet there are few Cantons richer in architectural interests than this, the smallest Canton in Switzerland.

The Zugersee was intensively settled in the stone age as is proved by the many remnants of the lake dwellings which have been discovered. The Romans settled in or near the town. In the fifth and seventh centuries the Germanic tribes began to settle in the region. Zug was the place of the assembly for the Austrian armies on their way to defeat at Morgarten in 1315. In 1352 Zug was besieged and captured by the Forest Canton with the assistance of the neighbouring citizens of the towns and villages of Aegeri, Baar and Menzingen. In the Italian campaigns of the sixteenth century Peter Kolin and Hans Schwarzmurer brought new lustre to the military prestige of the Swiss. In the religious civil wars Zug played a decisive rôle, for the critical battles were fought in or on the frontier of this little State.

Zug is not only a charming town with an immediate appeal to all lovers of the past, but it is equally attractive to lovers of lake and mountain scenery. The view from the lake shore is one of the finest in the Alps. Framed between the mighty slope of the Rigi, and the lesser range on the right, we can see the distant snows of the Wetterhorn and Eiger. This view, in which there is a perfect balance between the great peaks and the lesser ranges, is the theme of one of Calame's loveliest paintings.

2. Old Buildings in Zug

Let us begin our explorations of Zug in the Untergasse, just above the lake, an important commercial centre in the days when merchandise destined for Italy, via the St. Gotthard, was transferred at Zug from carriages to the lake boats.   As we turn off from the Fischmarkt into the Untergasse, we notice at the corner the Rathaus.   The Rathaus was built in 1505 and rebuilt in 1617.   The three top stories provide an excellent example of late Gothic windows.   The slender columns in the windows serve no functional purpose for the arches are carried on supports invisible from the exterior.   Don't fail to visit the Gothic hall on the third floor and note the charming tendril theme in the carving over the north window, and David Pfau's Stove (1699) in the little Ratsaal.

Let us stroll down this street looking first at the houses on the north side and then retracing our steps to examine the southern side of the street, nearest to the lake.

Haus No. 9 is rather charming.   It was rebuilt in 1526. Then comes Haus No. 11 (1528), " Schwanen " (1494) with a very attractive door which dates from 1779. The last house is the Provisorhaus.

The lower side of the street is the more attractive.   Facing us as we come out of the Untergasse is the west side of the Liebfrauenkapelle, next to which is " Seehof " (1712), and now turn back down the Untergasse and you pass Haus No. 24 (1563), the Schönbrunnerhaus (1521) and the Fischerstube, No. 12, which was built in 1487.   A little passage between the Fischerstube and the adjoining house (once a " Sust," where merchandise was transferred from the road to the lake boats) leads down to the lake.   No. 10 is the Haus Reg. Rat Meyer (1527) and No. 4 at the corner, the Huns Zinngiesser Keiser.   This bleak catalogue

can, of course, give no idea of the charm of this mediaeval
street. You could spend a month in Zug without exhausting the interest of its old buildings. The limits of my
space confine me to a few suggestions.

However hurried your visit you should try to see the
Mint at the corner of the Zeughausgasse and to obtain
permission to visit the Zurlaubenhof just below St. Michael's
Church, which was built towards the close of the sixteenth
century. The Zurlaubens were perhaps the most famous
of the Zug families, justly proud of their military record.
The great Hall is decorated with interesting mural
paintings.

3. Churches in Zug

The old parish church of St. Michael was pulled down
in 1898, one of the last and worst acts of vandalism of which
the most vandalistic of all centuries was guilty, but Zug
was better able to endure the loss than most towns would
have been for it possesses in St. Oswald's the finest Gothic
parish church in Switzerland. I have not been able to
discover why the cult of St. Oswald took root in Zug in
the early fourteenth century. St. Oswald, King of
Northumbria from 633 to 641 A.D., was brought up in
exile by the monks of Iona, and remained throughout life
a fervent Christian. He defeated Cadwallon at Rowley
Burn near Hexham, fighting within sight of the cross
which he had erected before the fight. According to
Bede, before battle he offered up a prayer for " victory
in the just war which we have undertaken for the delivery
of our people." St. Oswald's Church at Zug was begun
in 1478. The Gothic sculpture on the exterior, and the
paintings in the interior, would entitle this church to rank
among the most famous parish churches in Europe.

If you have time you should also try to visit the Kapuziner-
kloster, the Convent of Maria Opferung with the enchanting
fountain (1698) in the courtyard, and the Kapelle St.

Konrad (1623). A visit to the Liebfrauenkapelle can be combined with your stroll through the Untergasse, which leads to this chapel, the stained glass of which has now been removed to the museum in Zug, which you must not fail to visit. It is tantalising to be limited by space to the bleakest notes of the churches and famous buildings of Zug. I should like, for instance, to describe in detail the lovely fountains for which Zug is famous. Let me recommend the visitor who is wise enough to spend a few weeks in Zug to persuade his host to obtain from the cantonal library the loan of Dr. Linus Birchler's classic work *Die Kunstdenkmäler des Kantons Zug*.

4. Goethe at Zug

Goethe spent a night at Zug in 1797. He stayed at the Hotel Ochsen and fortunately some of the stained-glass windows he so much admired are still to be seen at the Ochsen. John Winn wandered round Switzerland after Waterloo and bought up at ridiculous prices the stained-glass panes which the Swiss, who had been impoverished by the Napoleonic wars, were only too glad to sell. Many of the best examples of this local art from Zug found their way into Nortell Priory near Wakefield in Yorkshire, including, very probably, the rest of the stained glass which Goethe admired in the Hotel Ochsen at Zug.

I am grateful to Dr. Koch for calling my attention to this interesting link between England and Zug.

Some of my happiest days at Zug were spent on the lake itself. People who are for ever complaining that Switzerland is overrun by trippers should appreciate the Zug steamers whose modest tonnage disclaims by implication any ambition to cater for the " personally conducted." Indeed, the only passengers I ever met on these steamers were Swiss.

Nobody would pretend that the scenery is as majestic as that of Lake Lucerne, and yet it has its own intimate charm, and I was pleased to find that I am not alone in my belief that this unpretentious lake has an appeal which is perhaps easier to convey than to analyse, for Mr. John Russell, whose appreciation of mountain architecture is as cool as his enthusiasm for baroque architecture is exuberant, pays a discerning tribute to this little lake, " to me infinitely more congenial," he writes, " than the lake of Como. I have few Swiss memories more happy than that of bathing in the warm waters of this disregarded and rather featureless mere. Barefoot among the apple orchards, or adrift upon the unbroken surface of the lake, I would not have exchanged my situation for any other in the world."

Chapter XX

THE ST. GOTTHARD FROM FLÜELEN TO GÖSCHENEN

1. Brunnen to Flüelen

THE Axenstrasse by which the motorist travels from Brunnen to Flüelen was first tunnelled out of the rock between 1863 and 1865. Before then there was no road connection between Flüelen and Brunnen, and it was this fact, as we shall see, which rendered the St. Gotthard useless as a military road.

The steamer from Brunnen to Flüelen calls at the steamer station of Tellsplatte, Tell's Chapel ("where Tell preached," according to the ribald Mark Twain). The original chapel was erected in 1388 on the spot where Tell sprang out of the boat which was carrying him to captivity.

Flüelen is the last port on the lake, and a station on the St. Gotthard line. The charming little château of Rudenz, just beyond the church, once belonged to the Attinghausen family which played such an important rôle in the fight for Swiss independence. The road from Flüelen to the St. Gotthard via Altdorf and Andermatt will be described in the section on Altdorf.

Before leaving the lake, let us recall the past history of these lake steamers which serve us so well. I commend to the reader *The Lake of Lucerne—Its Ships and Passengers*, by Captain J. Bachmann, who was for many years captain of one of the lake steamers. This booklet may be obtainable in Lucerne bookshops, or the Lucerne Steamship Company might be able to produce a copy. According to Captain Bachmann, navigation between Lucerne and Uri was controlled by guilds, " The St. Nicholas Societies," who were granted by the local authorities the sole right to convey people and goods.

In 1820 the road over the St. Gotthard was built and the traffic on the lake was still further increased by the growing fashion for mountain scenery. The old rowing boat was doomed by the advent of steam.

On December 1st, 1835, the house of Knorr in Lucerne founded a steamship company. Their first steamer, *Stadt Lucerne*, was about 103 feet long, and 20 feet broad with 150 horse-power engine. It carried a massive mast so as to reinforce the engine by means of a sail when the wind was favourable. The ship's boiler was heated with fir and beechwood and the steamer could convey three hundred people. The first trip by this new paddle steamer took place on September 20th, 1836. The shores of the lake were lined with excited spectators. The new company was bitterly opposed by the boatmen of the old companies, but of course in vain. A second and rival company started regular trips on January 1st, 1848, and, as a result of the competition between the two companies, a first-class return ticket from Lucerne to Flüelen and back (thirty miles each way) cost fifty centimes and a second-class a mere thirty, rather less than a penny for *ten* miles at the current rate of exchange.

Flüelen lost much of its importance after the Axenstrasse had been built, for until the road to Brunnen was constructed, all travellers had to continue their journey from Flüelen by boat and it was therefore convenient to break the journey at Flüelen where the change over from road to lake took place. Before the age of steam oarsmen would calculate on covering two to three miles an hour and up to six miles an hour with a good wind. On land a traveller would average about twenty-five miles a day but a baggage train, particularly for a person of importance, would take about three times as long. Curiously enough the relative speeds of passenger and goods traffic was about the same in the Middle Ages as to-day, when goods trains average about twenty miles an hour as against sixty miles for an express train.

2. Altdorf

About two miles beyond Flüelen we reach Altdorf (1,518 ft.), the capital of the Canton of Uri, and the traditional scene of William Tell's demonstration of archery (see page 32). The main square is adorned by Kissling's monument (1895) to Tell. The old tower may date from the fifth century. The historical museum is worth a visit. Suvoroff, whose Alpine campaign is described in the next chapter, spent a night at Altdorf. A memorial tablet on the Jauch mansion marks the site of his headquarters. Schiller mentions the forest above Altdorf (the Bannwald) which protects Altdorf from falling rocks and in which tree cutting is banned. In 1920 the forest was partly destroyed by an avalanche. Henry James' reaction to the patrician houses at Altdorf has already been quoted, page 181.

As the train leaves Altdorf we can see to the right the ruined castle of Attinghausen in which Baron Werner von Attinghausen, who appears in Schiller's play, died in 1320.

A fine motor road leads from Altdorf over the Klausen (6,437 ft.) pass to the Linthal and Glarus. Half an hour east of Altdorf on the Klausen road lies the little village of Bürglen, the traditional home of Tell. The chapel dates from 1582.

Engelberg can be reached in nine hours from Altdorf over the stony and not particularly interesting Surenen Pass (7,560 ft.).

3. Amsteg and Göschenen

Four miles beyond Altdorf we reach Erstfeld (1,558 ft.), at the foot of the Erstfelder-Tal whence the Spannort

peaks can be climbed or crossed to Engelberg. Amsteg
(1,712 ft.) lies at the foot of the beautiful Maderanertal, a
visit to which is described in the next chapter. The next
section of the railway line is a joy to children whose elders
have taken care to point out to them the little church of
Wassen on its first appearance. Owing to curves and
loops of the line, this little church seems subject to a
succession of magic bilocations, sometimes appearing to the
right and sometimes to the left of the train. Twenty-three
miles from Altdorf we reach Göschenen at the entrance of
the St. Gotthard tunnel.

The name Göschenen (formerly Geschenen) provides
evidence of Italian influence. It is derived from the
Ticinese-Italian word *cascina*, which is the equivalent of
Sennhüte, the huts inhabited by the " Senn " who look
after the cattle on the grazing alps. Geschinen, at the
opening of the Nufenan Pass into the Rhone valley and
" in der Geschina," near Brig at the end of the old Simplon
road, are derived from the same word. As are also Gesch
near Neidergestelen and Gescheli near Silenen in
Canton Uri.

From Göschenen a rack-and-pinion railway leads
through the famous Schöllenen Gorge to Andermatt and
thence to the St. Gotthard Pass.

From Göschenen (3,640 ft.) a good path leads in three
hours to the Göschener Alp (5,625 ft.). The peaks which
can be climbed from the Hotel Dammagletcher are not as
high or as famous as the Matterhorn or Mont Blanc or
Finsteraarhorn, but the Dammastock (11,920 ft.) and the
Sustenhorn (11,523 ft.) are excellent peaks on which to
matriculate, and those who are in search of exceptionally
difficult rock climbs will find plenty to occupy them if
they make the comfortable Hotel Dammagletscher their
headquarters.

N

Chapter XXI

"STOCKINGS WITH SHORTS"

WE met at Amsteg my friend Herr Mengelt whose praise is in the preface of this book, and his secretary, Fraulein Heusser, who had come from Lucerne, whereas I had caught the first train from Andermatt. We breakfasted at the Stern, one of those old coaching inns which lost much of their custom when the railway was built and regained much that was lost when the motoring age began. The old prints and old furniture evoked the Switzerland whose beauty had not been tarnished by the Industrial Revolution.

The first part of our journey up the Maderanertal was by coach, but most of the climb is on foot unless you can get a lift, as we did on the descent, in the hotel jeep. We were more than ready for lunch when we reached the admirable Hotel-Pension zum Schweizer Alpenclub (4,442 ft.).

The Landammann of Uri who owns the hotel asked me to vet the English of a notice distributed to all his guests which ran as follows:—

> *We beg to omit summer clothes of extremity.*
> *Nobody will object on bare legs of even bigger boys, but gentlemen ought to wear for their own advantage stockings with shorts.*
> *However, we appeal especially at the good taste of our honourable guests, in first of all to ladies about their garments too.*

" Is that quite correct? " he asked.

" Perfect," I replied. " I wouldn't alter a word."

After lunch my host took me for a walk. We passed a notice board informing the visitors that their dress should conform to the moral standards of the mountain people. " *Wenn Shortsch dann Strümfe.* " I asked my host whether any microbes of modern thought ever penetrated into the Maderanertal. He looked grave, as well he might for two of the herdsmen had spent a week in Zürich the previous summer and had returned with their heads chock full of nonsense.

It is the custom in the Maderanertal for the herdsmen to sing a hymn to Our Lady as the sun sets, but the young men who had met the twentieth century at Zürich announced that such rustic pieties belonged to a world which was vanishing. And so alas! the music of the ancient chant no longer rose from their particular Alp at sunset. " But they soon learned sense," said my host.

" What do you mean? " I asked.

" Oh well, it happened like this. One night they were woken from their sleep by the bellowings of their cows. They got up and discovered that many of their cows were no longer on their grazing grounds and that the agitated mooing came from far above, for the cows were stuck on rocky ground and could not get down without help and in trying to get them down next morning three were killed. And after that," my host added, " we had no more nonsense and the night prayers were said as before."

" Of course," said I, " I am delighted that the two herdsmen should have resumed their night prayers but I can't help feeling that it is a pity that so fine a miracle should have been wasted on a pious Catholic valley."

" Wasted? " replied the Landammann, obviously nettled by the implied suggestion that the Maderanertal had not such a good claim as Lourdes or Fatima as the setting for a supernatural manifestation, and of course he was right, but Stalin doesn't say his night prayers either, and the Atom War might be avoided if Stalin were awoken from his slumbers by the bellowing of Politburo members **impaled** on the domes of the Kremlin. More could be achieved, I feel, by displaced Commissars than by displaced cows.

The Maderanertal is famous for the variety of its climbs and for the beauty of its waterfalls. I remembered those lines in Tennyson's *Lotus Eaters* which were inspired by Lauterbrunnen.

> A land of streams! some, like a downward smoke
> Slow-dropping veils of thinnest lawn, did go;
> And some thru' wavering lights and shadows broke
> Rolling, a slumbrous sheet of foam below.

I asked the Landammann if he knew the Staubbach at Lauterbrunnen. Yes, he had seen it and I gathered that he thought that it wasn't too bad as Bernese waterfalls go.

Berne and Uri meet on the summit of the Susten Pass. The old bridle path was built as a military route when Switzerland was threatened by Napoleon, and the modern superb road when Switzerland was preparing for a German invasion. " The Uri men," said my old friend Max Amstutz, who drove me to the top of the Susten, " never finished their part of the road. The Bernese were so anxious to complete this road that they stretched a point and built down from the top of the pass towards Uri. I bet those Urners won't pay their proper share either." I was amused by this eruption of Bernese chauvinism and still more amused by the Landammann's reaction when I quoted this conversation. In the general interests of culture every effort should be made to aggravate regional rivalries. I felt I had done my bit by reporting Max's Urnerphobia to the Landammann of Uri.

Those hours which I spent in the Maderanertal reinforced my gratitude to the great mountain mission of separation. It is because mountains keep men *apart* that they are the true friends of culture, for all culture is regional in its source and religious in its inspiration. Secularism,

centralisation and mechanisation are the three great
enemies of culture.

The secularist lives in the three dimensional world of
matter, but all great art and poetry is born in that fourth
dimension of the spirit. As religion fades, the creative
genius of man finds expression no longer in art or in song
but in engineering. You need not subscribe to any
particular religion to believe this. You need only be
gifted with historical discernment. Spengler was a vague
pantheist but Spengler writes:—

" Culture is ever synonymous with religious creativeness.
Every great culture begins with a mighty theme that rises
out of the pre-urban countryside, is carried through in the
cities of art and intellect and closes with a finale of
materialism in the world cities."

Cyril Conolly, writing under the pseudonym of Palinurus,
says, " There are millions like me . . . pagans living by
christian morals . . . unsatisfied materialists " and then
adds, " To-day our literature is suffering from the decay of
poetry and decline of fiction . . . let us consider if there is
any living writer whose silence we should consider a literary
disaster, who with three centuries more of art and history to
draw from can sustain comparison with, for example,
Pascal." Goethe was in the main an agnostic but Goethe
was convinced that " Men will continue to be creative in
poetry and art only so long as there are religions. After
that they merely imitate and repeat, as is our case with
regard to antiquity. All the monuments of the ancient
world were created as means of faith and we imitate them
to indulge and gratify nothing but our fancy."

The second great enemy of culture is the machine. In
the great manufacturing centres, as Matthew Arnold
points out, " man's instinct for beauty and man's instinct
for fit and pleasing forms of social life and manners find
little or no satisfaction."

More than a hundred years have passed since Michelet

foresaw the consequence of the Industrial Revolution. " The machine," he wrote, " enslaves the gesture of the workman and suppresses artistic research. The machine extends its empire over social life and introduces automatism even in the realm of thought. In the name of the philosophy of the state the machine merges the individual in the mob and solitary reflection disappears. The State divorced from the fatherland, industry and literature divorced from art, humanity divorced from man, *voilà à quoi aboutit le mechanisme.*"*

In the churches of central Switzerland, as elsewhere, you can trace the destructive influence of mechanisation in the realm of religious art. Before photography and other mechanical contrivances for the reproduction and mass distribution of works of art were invented every artist relied on his own inspiration and tradition. Altarpieces and paintings in the pre-industrial age were often crude but they were never vulgar or insipid, and never lacked the signmark of creative thought.

In the second half of the nineteenth century German publishers began to flood Switzerland with mass-produced prints of sentimental religious paintings with the result that the influence of mass production, an invention of the machine age, can be studied in many of the churches of central Switzerland. The local craftsman no longer needed to rely on his inventive faculty. There was plenty to copy but nothing worth copying. And of course the local Catholic communities were no longer dependent on local craftsmen, for they could order their coloured prints of Teutonic Christs or those ghastly mass-produced statues of the Sacred Heart from the nearest ecclesiastical shop.

But the main enemy of culture is not the machine or industrialism but secularism. The chief monument of the secular philosophy of our age is the building designed as a parliament for that League of Nations which was as

* " Behold what mechanism leads to "; quoted from *Le Peuple*.

tragic in its failure and collapse as the Tower of Babel. The artists who covered the walls of this building with frescoes scrupulously refrained from the slightest hint of man's eternal destiny. It is a strictly secular and three-dimensional humanism which is represented in those portentous frescoes of heroic workmen discarding their fetters and saluting the rosy dawn of peace and progress. But it was the morning star of Mars which watched over the final sunset of those dawnist illusions.

The contrast which Mr. John Russell, from whose delightful descriptions of Einsiedeln I shall quote, draws between the League of Nations building and the Abbey of Einsiedeln cannot be explained by religious loyalties, for Mr. Russell makes it clear that he has no violent prejudice against and no particular faith in any form of institutional religion, but he perceives that great architecture, like great poetry, has its roots in that fourth dimension which the secularists deny. Einsiedeln, he tells us, " was the natural product of a generation in which everyone—architects, builders, sculptor and painter—spoke the same flexible and infinitely suggestible language. One could not even conceive of a similar successful church being built to-day; as for the League of Nations building—in some ways the secular counterpart of this abbey—I need only mention its name to bring before the reader a chaos of futile expenditure."

Chapter XXII

ANDERMATT AND THE ST. GOTTHARD PASS

IN the old coaching days Andermatt's main importance was as a halting place in which to spend the night before or after crossing the St. Gotthard. The opening of the St. Gotthard tunnel in 1882 naturally reduced the traffic across the pass but the motoring age restored much of its old importance to Andermatt. To the mountaineer, Andermatt (4,737 ft.) is an admirable centre particularly for those who are serving an apprenticeship as guideless climbers, for there is excellent rock and ice work in the region. The comparatively moderate height of the mountains would make Andermatt an ideal centre for an Alpine meet restricted to comparative novices. Andermatt is also a famous ski-ing centre, headquarters of the White Hare Club, and the place chosen for the first Junior British Championship.

The name of the Urseren valley in which Andermatt lies is derived from the Latin *Ursus* a bear, and *Ursarii* bear hunters. The first documentary reference to this valley which survives refers to Ursenberg (1236) and later to Ursarn (1285).

Urseren once belonged to the province of Rhaetia. Its inhabitants were converted to Christianity in the seventh century probably by monks from the great Abbey of Disentis on the other side of the Oberalp Pass. The Abbey was founded in 614. The little church of St. Columban near the entrance to the Urner Loch is mentioned in the will of Bishop Tells of Coire as early as 766, but the present structure is late-Gothic. Until the fourteenth century Urseren belonged to the Holy Roman Empire and it was only in 1410 that the Urseren valley was incorporated in the Canton of Uri. The village of " An der Matten " is mentioned in a document of 1309. The church of St. Columban marks the site of an earlier settlement known as " Zu Kilchen."

1. The History of the St. Gotthard Pass

The most important event in the history of the valley was the opening of the route through the Schöllenen gorge towards the end of the thirteenth century (*circa* 1290). In order to open the gorge to traffic a bridge had to be built across the river (Teufelsbrücke, Devil's Bridge), but this was not the most serious obstacle. Just before the Schöllenen railway line reaches Andermatt it skirts the smooth limestone rocks just above the torrent by means of an iron bridge whose position is very similar to that of the old Twärenbrücke, the erection of which, towards the end of the thirteenth century, first made it possible for travellers to reach Andermatt via the Schöllenen gorge.

In the smooth rocks underneath the rail can be seen a few holes about an inch in circumference, in two rows, the lower of which is about ten feet above the level of the torrent. Some remnants of iron rings can still be detected on the face of the cliff.

In the years 1707 to 1708 the inside of the cliff, on the outside of which hung the Twärenbrücke, was tunnelled by a Tessiner engineer, Pietro Moretini by name. This tunnel, the Urnerloch, robbed the Schöllenen gorge of much of its terrors.

Every Swiss historian that I had read before visiting Andermatt stated that the St. Gotthard was " opened " towards the end of the thirteenth century, from which I assume either that these distinguished historians were not themselves very familiar with the Andermatt region or lacked the experience and the eye of a mountaineer. A mountaineer's first thought on entering the Schöllenen gorge would be to speculate on the possibilities of evading the gorge by a detour. On arriving at Andermatt in 1949 it struck me that the Bäzberg would provide an easy alternative to the gorge and, on making inquiries, I was assured that remnants of an old bridge path could still be discerned across the Bäzberg and from the foot of the Bäzberg to Hospental. After completing this chapter I received from the National Library at Berne some pamphlets about the St. Gotthard which confirms what I had heard at Andermatt. Dr. Laur-Belart in his *Studien zur Eröffnungegeschicte des Gotthardpasses*, and Dr. Jacob Escher-Bürkli in *Von der alten Gotthardstrasse*, arrive at very similar conclusions.

There are five ways in which the Reuss valley could be reached from Andermatt without passing through the Schöllenen gorge, the Fellilücke (2,480 metres),* and the depression (2,100 metres)* between Gütsch and Stock, both leading from Oberalp just above Andermatt. (We know that mules often used the latter pass, as, for instance, in 1640 when the bridge in the Schöllenen gorge had been swept away by a flood.) A longer route via the Alpiglenlücke (2,778 metres),* which involves crossing some glacier névé, connected the Andermatt valley with the Göschener alp from time immemorial. The most direct route over the lower shoulder of the Bäzberg would have presented formidable difficulties to the building of a mule path, and the route which was almost certainly followed before the Schöllenen gorge was rendered practicable for traffic, led over a higher shoulder of the Bäzberg under the Spitze (2,210 metres).*

This détour involved an additional 2,500 feet of climbing, and of course also of descent, compared with the direct route through the Schöllenen, an addition of about four to five hours. It was only after the short cut through the Schöllenen had been engineered that the St. Gotthard

* I give these heights in metres as map references.

proved to be a shorter route into Italy than the Lukmanier, with consequences for the future history of Switzerland that have been explained in Chapters III and IV.

Though the pass was certainly crossed in Roman times, it never became a great military pass. The détour to dodge the Schöllenen gorge was no greater objection to the St. Gotthard than the détour which the Romans cheerfully followed to dodge the Via Mala was to the Splügen. The fatal objection to the St. Gotthard was the fact that there was no road from Flüelen to Brunnen, and insufficient boats to transport an army, as indeed Suvoroff was to discover at a much later date.

No historian with any mountaineering experience could possibly make the mistake of assuming that an easy range could only be crossed at one point. The mountaineer would instinctively expect to find many alternative routes which would avoid the Schöllenen gorge.

From Andermatt an almost level road leads in a mile and a half to Hospental, known to the Romans as Hospitaculum. Queen Victoria made a long stay at the Meyerhof, a charming hotel which combines a period charm with modern comfort. Some of Herr Meyer's ancestors, direct and collateral, served in Spain and he showed me some of their journals and a lovely sofa which a Colonel Meyer had brought back from Spain.

The St. Gotthard pass is about 2,000 feet above and about five miles from Hospental. The first certain reference to the pass occurs in a manuscript dated 1236, when the pass is referred to under the name of Mons Elvelinus, " which the Lombards call Ursare " (Ursern). The name St. Gotthard is first found in the enumeration of the great Habsburg possessions drawn up in the first year of the fourteenth century. The mule-path is first mentioned in 1293, and the hospice on the summit in 1331. In the fourteenth century the pass was certainly well known. It was the chief route through which merchandise passed from Germany across Switzerland into Italy, and in the fifteenth century it facilitated the conquest by the Swiss of the Italian bailiwicks.

It was not until 1820–30 that the carriage-road was constructed over the pass, and the great railway-tunnel under the pass was not opened to traffic until 1882.

The pass was called after Gotthard (960–1038) or Godehard Bishop of Hildesheim, who was canonized under the name of St. Gotthard in 1132.

The French troops were stationed on the pass during the winter of 1798–1799, and broke up the old hospice for firewood.

2. Suvoroff and the St. Gotthard

In 1798, the French Revolutionary army overran Switzerland. At the end of February 1799 the Austrians and their Russian allies entered Switzerland hoping to cut the communications between the French armies and Italy. On June 5th–6th, 1799, the Austrians won the first battle of Zürich, but the Austro-Russian coalition was weakened by disagreements. The Austrians recrossed the Rhine with the result that the Russian General Korsakof was crushed by Masséna at the second battle of Zürich on September 26th. When Suvoroff, who was in Italy, heard the news of this defeat he resolved to march his army across the Alps. He fought his first battle near the summit of the St. Gotthard, defeating a division of the French army on September 24th, 1799.

Suvoroff was a genius, with the contempt of a genius for orthodox strategy and behaviour. Mr. William Wickham,* who was sent on a special mission to the allies by Lord Granville, was impressed by Suvoroff's audacity, and faintly shocked by his methods, for he allowed his men to loot and plunder as they pleased. " The elements of which the Russian troops are composed,"

* See page 54

he wrote, " are such that, when put together, they cannot be called an *army* in any respect but the number of men." Suvoroff was a great admirer both of English beer and of English forthrightness. " *C'est un vrai God Damn!* " he exclaimed while he read Wickham's first despatch.

After defeating the French on the St. Gotthard he hunted them down through the Schöllenen Gorge. The retreating French destroyed the Devil's Bridge, but a rough substitute bridge was hastily constructed out of planks and tied together with officers' sashes. The first heroic attempts to cross under heavy fire failed, and men and horses plunged into the torrent below. Major Mestchersky, the first officer to cross, was mortally wounded as he reached the other side. " Don't forget to mention me in despatches " were his last words.

In those days there was no Axenstrasse connecting Altdorf with Brunnen and there were insufficient boats to transport an army. Suvoroff, therefore, crossed the Kinzig-Kulm Pass (6,810 ft.) from Altdorf (1,518 ft.), a climb of over 5,000 feet. His men were so exhausted that they failed to carry the entrance to the Muotatal (1,995 ft.) and, turning east, crossed the Pragel Pass (5,060 ft.) to Glarus (1,559 ft.), finally reaching winter quarters in the Grisons by way of the Panixer Pass (7,897 ft.) on which the first of the October snows had already fallen.

In the course of crossing these four passes his army ascended an aggregate of over 20,000 feet, two-thirds the height of Everest. There is no parallel to Suvoroff's mountain campaign in Europe, but the great range of the Andes witnessed some equally remarkable campaigns during the South American wars of liberation. A tablet in the Schöllenen Gorge records Suvoroff's campaign. In 1945 the gilt lettering was hastily polished up in anticipation of a visit from high Russian officers who were then in Switzerland.

3. Historic Highways

Andermatt lies at the junction of two historic highways,
the St. Gotthard which runs from north to south, and the
great route which leads from Brig, in the Rhone valley,
across the Furka pass to Andermatt and thence across the
Oberalp pass to Disentis and Coire.

You can travel without changing carriages from Zermatt
via Brig to Andermatt and thence via Coire to St. Moritz.

Andermatt is not only a wonderful walking and ski-ing
centre, but a perfect base for exploring a historic region.
It is easy to visit Gletsch at the foot of the Rhone glacier
in the afternoon or, alternatively, to take the train to
Disentis and visit the magnificent Benedictine Abbey.
Father Placidus à Spescha, the father of purely sporting
mountaineering and the first man to make a regular
practice of climbing, year after year, was a monk at
Disentis. He was born in 1752 and died at the age of
eighty-two.

If you have come to Andermatt in your own car you
should not hurry away. A splendid day's motoring is to
cross the Oberalp (6,720 ft.) to Disentis (3,760 ft.) and
the Lukmanier (6,280 ft.) to Biasca, and thence return to
Andermatt via the St. Gotthard, a round tour of just a
hundred miles.

4. The Recurring Pattern

During my last visit to Andermatt I stayed at the
Monopole, and I spent a most interesting evening in the
private home of the proprietor, Herr Müller. His uncle,
who emigrated to America, became a famous portrait
painter. He was usually referred to as " the Italian
painter " because he was born in Italian Switzerland, in
Airolo to be precise, but he did what he could to remind
people of his Swiss origin by adding *Ury* to his name. He
painted the last three Popes, the Kaiser and the portrait

of Wilson which hangs in the Palace of the League of Nations.

Herr Müller, who belongs to one of the oldest of Urseren families, showed me proclamations and posters and old bills dating from the period when the French Revolutionary troops overran Switzerland. The Catholic peasantry were forced to date their bills in accordance with the revolutionary calendar, Thermidor, Fructidor, etc., but I suspect that this heretical dating caused them less worry than the fact that the bills were probably never paid. The French invented the modern technique, adopted by the Russians, of camouflaging annexation as liberation, and of exploiting the great word " Freedom " to destroy freedom.

Herr Müller showed me a proclamation issued by a Swiss Quisling warning the Swiss to disregard the promises of liberation made by the Austrian Kaiser. Substitute " American President " for " Austrian Kaiser " and the proclamation could have been used, with little alteration, by the North Korean Communists. " *Glaubt die Regierung liebt euch, and unsere Verfassung beglückt euch. Last es auf die Probe kommen.*" " Have faith in the government which loves you and in our constitution which will bring you fortune. Give us a trial." And then follow the usual threats of reprisals against any village foolish enough to distrust the " new order."

Again, it was the French Revolution which invented the propaganda technique of claiming apostolic descent from local heroes famous as the liberators of their country under foreign oppressors. Thus the French did not compare themselves to the Habsburgs, those earlier invaders of the Forest Cantons, but to the three patriarchs who swore an oath at Rütli to liberate their country from the proto- types of the French invaders. Herr Müller showed me a proclamation with a picture of William Tell and the propa- ganda slogan *Freyheit, Gleichheit* (" Freedom, Equality ") and another proclamation, adorned with a picture of the Rütli patriarchs, and signed by a Swiss Quisling, von Essingen, a Bernese name. There is a familiar ring about *Volks-Representant* and *Commissair*. There is a recurring pattern in the history of human tyranny—and of human folly. If our statesmen had read Burke on the French Revolution and remembered his warning, " There is no safety for honest men, but by believing all possible evil of evil men, and by acting with promptitude, decision and steadiness on that belief," there would have been no necessity for the air lift to Berlin, and there would have been no war in Korea.

ANDERMATT
looking towards the Furka

Othmar Baur, Einsiedeln

EINSIEDELN
looking down the Nave
(Gnadenkapelle in background)

Chapter XXIII

EINSIEDELN

EINSIEDELN (2,895 ft.), which lies in hilly country between the Lakes of Lucerne and Zürich, is perhaps the most famous place of pilgrimage north of the Alps.

1. St. Meinrad

The founder, St. Meinrad, a Hohenzollern by race, some time after entering the Benedictine community at Bollingen, left them in search of a severer retreat. His first cell was on the slopes of the Etzel above the eastern end of Lake Zürich. When he resolved to find a new cell he walked past the marshy swamp of Sihl towards a forest, and paused at a clearing between trees, down which gushed a little stream, and here he made his dwelling and built a small oratory and hut. Here he lived for some years, his only companions being two ravens which he had tamed. Then one day two robbers broke in upon his solitude and murdered him for the sake of the hidden store of wealth which they believed him to have amassed. They found no hidden treasure, and left in disgust, pursued by the two ravens whose persistent attentions to the robbers attracted the notice of the magistrates at Zürich. The robbers were cross-examined and confessed. They were finally broken on the wheel. The seal of Einsiedeln Abbey is adorned by two ravens to this day.

St. Meinrad was murdered in 861. His little oratory was preserved as a shrine, and in 934 Eberhard, the first Abbot of the Benedictine community which had settled there, built round this cell the first church, and round the church the first Abbey. In September, 948, Conrad, Bishop of Constance, was invited to consecrate St. Meinrad's chapel.

On the night before the consecration was to take place the Bishop went into the church to pray and heard angelic voices singing the words of the consecration service. It was therefore with natural reluctance that Conrad began the consecration service. As he did so, a voice was heard— *Frater, cessa, divinitus consecrata est* (Cease, brother, for this chapel has been consecrated).

It was at a much later date that the " Black Virgin " was added to the chapel. The statue is late Gothic, its origin south Germany. The colour is usually explained as the result of candle smoke, but is more probably due to that tendency to abstraction which is normal in statues and pictures believed to be miraculous. Many miraculous statues are black, as Dr. Linus Birchler has pointed out (*Gnadenbilder—im Jahrbuch der Renaissance*, 1924).

During the French invasion the Black Madonna was removed and hidden in Tirol. During the flight the statue suffered from damp, and was repainted black by Johann Fuetscher in Blumenegg (Vorarlberg), for the faithful would have been perplexed had the sacred statue not been black.

The modern Abbey is the sixth to occupy the present site, three of its predecessors having been burnt. The late Gothic style in which the fifth Abbey was rebuilt is shown in Meryan's *Topographia Helvetiae*. In 1703 the Chapter resolved to rebuild the Abbey, and what was left of the Abbey as depicted by Meryan was finally pulled down in 1719.

The principal architect of the present Abbey, Caspar Moosbrugger, was a Bavarian who was born in 1656, who entered the Monastery as a lay brother in 1682, and who died, after a long and successful career as an architect, in 1723. After his death the direction of the work was taken over by Brother Thomas Meyer. Caspar's brother Johann Moosbrugger, and Joseph Rueff, the builder of Engelberg, were in charge of many of the later operations.

The invading armies of revolutionary France pillaged
the Abbey and partially destroyed the Gnadenkapelle, but
the present chapel has much in common with the original
chapel as built by Solari, the architect of Salzburg Cathedral.

2. The Charm of Baroque

There are thousands of books of technical interest on
architecture, but very few, perhaps half a dozen at the
most, which are masterpieces of artistic interpretation.
Ruskin's chapter on the nature of Gothic in *The Stones of
Venice* was not only perhaps the noblest interpretation of
architecture in all literature, but the seed from which
flowered a masterpiece, the challenge which provoked
Geoffrey Scott to defend that architecture of the Renaissance which Ruskin never understood. You should read
Scott's *Architecture of Humanism* before leaving Einsiedeln or,
better still, carry it with you during your travels through
Central Switzerland, the Baroque lover's paradise.

It is as difficult to evoke the special characteristics of a
building as to differentiate in prose between the special
characteristics of different mountain scapes, but Geoffrey
Scott is as inspired in his interpretation of architecture as
Leslie Stephen in his evocation of mountain architecture.
Here, for instance, are some of the many passages in which
Geoffrey Scott defends and explains the attraction of
Baroque:—

> The baroque architects conceived of movement, tossing
> and returning; movement unrestrained, yet not destruc-
> tive of that essential repose which comes from composi-
> tion, nor exhaustive of that reserve of energy implied in
> masses, when, as here, they are truly and significantly
> massed. . . . Other architectures, by other names,
> have conveyed strength in repose. These styles may
> be yet grander, and of an interest more satisfying and
> profound. But the laughter of strength is expressed in
> one style only: the Italian baroque architecture of the
> seventeenth century.

Moreover, the great baroque masterpieces, the colonnade of St. Peter's and the Salute at Venice, not only achieve the " immediate merit of the picturesque," but also produce " a permanent impression of a broad serenity; for they have that baroque assurance which even baroque convulsion cannot rob of its repose."

3.   The Interior of the Abbey

My wife and I have the happiest memories of the Pfauen Hotel which faces the Abbey, the hotel in which Goethe stayed.   As I write, I can see, as we so often saw from our rooms at the Pfauen, the floodlit West Front of the Abbey, and the pilgrims returning with their lanterns from the hill near by with its impressive Stations of the Cross.

The Abbey dominates Einsiedeln like a great sea cliff, and the last ripples of the little town wash the shelving shore of the stone terraces which sweep up to the base of the West Front.   All the subtlety of Baroque finds expression in the perfect balance between the convex central façade and the concave stone arcades.

The Liebfrauenbrunnen below the terraces was erected in 1684 by Hans Keuen and renovated in 1893.   There is a constant procession of pilgrims wandering round the fountain and drinking at the fourteen bronze water spouts designed by Hans Füssli (1650 to 1727).   Let us climb the stone arcades and passing between Babel's statues of Kaiser Otto I and Henry II enter the great Abbey through the west door.

Facing us as we enter is the Gnadenkapelle (see page 211) which contains the miraculous statue of Our Lady.   Let us find some place in the nave where we can sit and rest and allow the majestic interior to assert its power over our minds.

Ruskin could see nothing in Baroque but the expression of pagan pride and pagan infidelity, but if he had spent as many days in Einsiedeln as he spent months in Venice he might have come to love Baroque almost as much as he loved Gothic, for Baroque has infinitely more in common with Byzantine and Gothic art and architecture than with the purer and more classical forms of Renaissance architecture. Classical architecture is as far less rich in ornamentation than Baroque and Gothic. The classical architecture excelled in the aesthetic exploitation of empty space and in the cult of simplicity, Byzantine, Gothic and Baroque craftsmen in the fertility of invention with which they filled their empty spaces or, as in the case of St. Mark's, Venice, covered the brick walls with incrusted marble and mosaic. There is, perhaps, something symbolic in the richness of Christian ornamentation at its best, for the *detail* of the Christian Revelation is as delightful as the detail of Greek polytheism is repulsive. We can only tolerate in modern galleries representations in stone or paint of disgusting myths such as Europa and the Bull, or Leda and the Swan because we have conditioned ourselves to enjoy as separate and discrete details the painting of Leda as a beautiful woman and the painting of a beautiful swan. Because classical polytheism is ethically repulsive and often aesthetically disgusting we turn with relief to the aesthetic simplicity of the Parthenon. The appeal of Greek architecture and art varies directly with its remoteness from the traditional polytheism of the society which built its noblest temples on the Acropolis, but it is the *detail* of the Christian Revelation which gives such infinite charm to the mosaics in St. Mark's, to the sculpture of Chartres and to the frescoes and statues of Einsiedeln. There is no incident in the Gospels, and no word spoken by Christ, which is not haunting in its beauty. The fertility of Byzantine, Gothic or Baroque inventiveness represents the inevitable response of artists, formed in the Christian tradition, to the inexhaustible recourses of a Revelation, as lovely in its detail as it is ennobling in its doctrine.

On your first visit to Einsiedeln you will almost certainly find the wealth of detail a little distracting. After spending some hours in the study of the church it is a relief to drop into the Abbey at night when the lights are subdued and detail lost in the deep shadows. At such times the High Altar alone emerges, a dim shape from the darkness, but there is a dance of wings where the subdued light plays on an angel suspended from pilaster or pulpit, and the subdued murmur of the pilgrims reciting the rosary provides an appropriate foil to the glimmer of Baroque ornamentation contending with the darkness.

It would be difficult to exaggerate the Abbey's debt to the brothers Assam (Kosmas Damian and Egid Quirin). These brothers, already famous for their work in South Germany, came to the Abbey in 1724 and remained for two years. Their decorations provide the perfect accompaniment to the structural melodies designed by Moosbrugger. "Unlike some of his successors," writes Mr. John Russell:

> E. Q. Assam always respected the overriding importance of Moosbrugger's outlines; for in these, and in the endless resonances of white and gold, the calling and answering of one perspective to another, and the mutual thrusting and yielding between one arch one dome, one gallery and its piers—in these relations, rather than in mere multiplication of grandeurs, does the genius of baroque reside. The art of the Assams is of a scrupulous but full-hearted sort. The two Bavarians were never abstract or intellectual in their approach; they were copious, sanguine, and disinhibited workmen, who spoke in direct, bodily terms of what they most enjoyed; and during their two years at Einsiedeln they perpetuated their robust and appreciative outlook in vista upon vista of compositions in which painting and decoration spoke the same language.

Moosbrugger was confronted with a problem of unusual delicacy when he was required to incorporate in the new church the Gnadenkapelle built on the site of St. Meinrad's cell. The chapel might so easily have seemed an awkward intrusion, but, as it is, the domed octagon seems as if pre-ordained to provide the perfect setting for the chapel, and the chapel itself has the organic relation of a primordial cell to the architectural structure by which it is enveloped. The theme of Assam's painting in the Octagon is the divine consecration of the chapel. One sees Bishop Conrad pausing as he hears the angelic voices. Christ and the Madonna, coming to the consecration, are represented in the west and east of the Octagon. There is a charming medallion of Charity by E. Q. Assam in the Octagon vault.

Even those who have little interest in art or in archi-tecture will brighten up when their attention is directed to the wrought iron screen which divides the nave from the choir and which is ingenious in its false perspective. The design is common in Switzerland. One meets it again at Disentis. This fine specimen of a not very exalted form of art is the work of Brother Jacob Nussbaumer who flourished towards the end of the seventeenth century.

The High Altar was sketched out by Gian Antonio Torricelli and executed by Pozzi, who made the statue of Our Lady on the Liebfraubrunnen in front of the church. It is perhaps salutary to be reminded in the Abbey of the tragic decline of all taste, ecclesiastical as well as secular, which set in during the nineteenth century. In 1880 Deschwanden was permitted to substitute for Franz Kraus' original paintings on the High Altar his own deplorable designs. Kraus' altar painting in the upper choir shows what we have lost by his untimely death. The Assumpta Galerie behind the High Altar is ornamented by four allegorical statues by J. B. Babel whose gift for what Mr. Russell calls " nonchalant grandeur " can be studied on the Klosterplatz.

The choir stalls in the upper choir by Michael Hartman of Lucerne are good specimens of seventeenth-century

Baroque, and the wall paintings by the brothers Toricelli of Lugano show a fluent and easy mastery of the Baroque idiom. Eight of the side altars are the work of Diego Carlone of Como who worked at Einsiedeln from 1730 to 1738.

Don't fail to visit the adjoining Beichtkirche, where confessions are heard, and which leads out of the north aisle of the church. The stucco work is by Pietro Nuerone (1680).

As the reader may now be presumed to be on his way home I will ask him to give one last look back to the Abbey before he returns to the Pfauen Hotel, to test his own reactions by those of Mr. Russell. The Klosterplatz, Mr. Russell writes:

is an essentially simple though cunning device for heightening the effect of the shallow incline which leads to the Abbey. One need not be an authority on style to sense how the eye is gathered in by the semi-circular arcades and swept through the gap, up the staircase and on to the façade of the church, where the architects have allowed themselves a certain elaboration and brilliance of detail in order to contain and satisfy our excitement. There is nothing particular in this, or in the skill with which the arcades, though vital to the general effect, never obtrude upon the main building. There is conscious art in the way in which, where everything else (even the flanking garden-walls) yields to the eye in a series of recessed curves, the entrance to the church bends suddenly outwards, and towards us, as if swollen by the splendours within. Yet these are the pleasures of geometry only—the few, telling horizontals of the staircase, and the sudden convergence of upward and downward lines upon the gap in the arcades. They would seem insufficient for so large a space if it were not for a factor which Moosbrugger can hardly have foreseen—the great gifts of Johann Baptist Babel. Babel came to Einsiedeln in 1746, when he was thirty-one, and worked there till his death in 1798. He is thought to have been a native of Augsburg. His statues on the Klosterplatz must have been his first large commission at Einsiedeln, and they embellish the west front of the abbey with something of the lavish humanity which we shall find in superabundance within the church. The Emperors Otto I and Heinrich II dominate the steps with a grandeur that is never tyrannical, and a conversational stance which Babel has extended even to Benno, the founder of the Abbey, as he stands above the garden gateway on the extreme right of the façade.

Of those who visit Einsiedeln very few discover the Abbey's magnificent collection of chalices and vestments, but most people insist on visiting the *Fürstensaal*, the hall of princes with its portraits of the Emperors Francis Joseph and William I, and of Napoleon III who presented the Abbey with the chandelier in the main church, which still advertises its donor's bad taste.

" Nature," said Sir Thomas Browne, " is the art of God," and at Einsiedeln the art of God is the perfect setting for the art of Man. The new artificial lake of Sihl is exactly what was needed as a foreground to the quiet charm of mountain ranges which make no attempt at dramatic effects and which seem somehow to have caught the serene note of the Benedictine *pax*. You should visit Etzel where St. Meinrad built his first cell and the little house beyond the bridge where the famous sixteenth-century doctor, Paracelsus, was born.

Do not hurry away from Einsiedeln. You will get very little out of the Abbey if you try to explore it in an afternoon. Even its aesthetic appeal cannot be absorbed in a few hours.

There may be some whose aesthetic reaction will be marred by their hatred of the religion of those who built Einsiedeln. A Marxist would, I suppose, feel very much as Gibbon felt when he visited the Abbey in 1775. " The title and worship of the Mother of God," he wrote,

" provoked my indignation; and the lively image of superstition suggested to me, as in the same place it had done to Zwingli, the most pressing argument for the reformation of the Church."

Gibbon hated everything which reminded him of the Church which he had joined for a few brief months. St. Mark's, Venice, he dismissed as " the worst architecture I ever saw." Confronted with a Gothic Cathedral he could only sniff, " I darted a contemptuous look on the stately monuments of superstition." Byzantine, Gothic or Baroque, it was all one to this arch philistine of the eighteenth century.

Goethe, on the other hand, was deeply moved by the clear evidence of mankind's " insatiable need for that same light and warmth," for that ever burning flame kindled by the " spark of sanctity and reverence " which once lit St. Meinrad's cell.

The modern world has lost Gibbon's confidence that the one cure for all our troubles is the suppression of what the eighteenth century meant by "enthusiasm." Among the thousands who take back with them from Einsiedeln a faith reinforced by immediate contact with the supernatural there are many who do not subscribe to all the doctrines of the Church of Rome.

No real Christian can fail to respond to the spiritual climate of Einsiedeln. Here, for instance, is a passage from a letter written from Einsiedeln by somebody who was not in communion with Rome. She begins with a description of the pilgrims walking in procession round the square:—

Last night as I watched them some words came into my mind—" Therefore with Angels and Archangels and with all the company of Heaven we laud and magnify Thy glorious Name." Truly in this beautiful place the dividing line between us and that other company does not seem so wide and deep. And as we kneel in St.

Meinrad's Shrine we beg for our own prayers to be
answered. Will we too receive the blessing for which we
beg? Surely it may be so here—above all other places
for it is one which has been consecrated by God.

. . . I think the people of Einsiedeln must be influenced
by the sanctity of the place. In all my travels I do
not think I have ever met such kindly service. As they
busy themselves in your employment that lovely Swiss
word Gern is often on their lips. It is best translated
by " gladly " or " with pleasure."

After dinner you walk back into the quiet church.
Before St. Meinrad's tomb the pilgrims still kneel in
supplication. The rest of the church is in darkness.
The only light comes from the Sanctuary Lamp shining
on the gold cross at the altar. And when you come out
of the church you see the wide expanse of sky as St.
Meinrad must often have seen it. Over the wooded
hill a silver moon is rising in a strangely deep blue sky.
Did he love that sweep of sky as we do? As we walk
back to the quiet hotel across the square the peace he
found is in our hearts too. Surely it is indeed holy
ground.

Few people whatever their faith can watch the daily
procession of the black-robed monks to the Gnadenkapelle without feeling that the one hope for this dis-
tracted planet is a world-wide rebirth of the Christian
dynamic. " Turn then, most gracious Advocate, thine
eyes of mercy towards us."

It was this same *Salve Regina* which the sailors of Columbus
sang every evening, lost as they believed themselves to be
in the wastes of the Atlantic. Here are the words which
the monks sing every afternoon before the Gnadenkapelle—

Salve, Regina, Mater misericordiae ; vita, dulcedo, et spes
nostra, salve. Ad te clamamus, exsules filii Hevae, ad te suspiramus,
gementes et flentes in hac lacrimarum valle. Eia ergo, advocata
nostra, illos tuos misericordes oculos ad nos converte ; et Jesum,
benedictum fructum ventris tui, nobis post hoc exilium ostende.
O clemens, o pia, o dulcis Virgo Maria.

APPENDIX

MOTORING DISTANCES IN MILES

(The figures in brackets indicate miles from the point of departure, and, where heights are given, heights above sea level. ABBREVIATIONS: m=miles; f=feet above sea level.)

1. THE APPROACHES TO CENTRAL SWITZERLAND

Basel—Olten (27 m)—Habsburg Castle, near Bad Schinznach (44 m)—Lucerne (77 m).

Basel—Olten (27 m)—Lucerne (65 m).

Delle—Porrentruy (9½ m)—Bienne (44 m)—Aarburg (54 m)— Berne (67 m)—Langnau (90 m)—Lucerne (126 m).

Delle—Moutier (34 m)—Via the Summit of Weissenstein, wonderful view, to Solothurn (48 m)—Berne (68 m)— Lucerne (127 m).

Pontarlier—Les Verrières (9½ m)—Neuchâtel (33 m)—Bienne (52 m)—Berne (75 m)—Lucerne (134 m).

Pontarlier—Vallorbes (16½ m)—Lausanne (50 m)—Morat (90 m)—Berne (107 m)—Lucerne (166 m).

2. THE MOTORING PASSES OF CENTRAL SWITZERLAND

Brünig

Lucerne (1,437 f)—Sarnen (1,555 f, 15 m)—Lungern (2,475 f, 25 m)—Brünig (3,317 f, 28 m)—Brienz (1,857 f, 35 m)— Interlaken (1,864 f, 45 m). Note: From Lucerne to Meiringen 33 miles.

Grimsel

Meiringen (1,960 f and 33 m from Lucerne via Brünig)— Innertkirchen, junction for Susten, see below (2,106 f, 3 m)— Grimsel Hospice (6,155 f, 17 m)—Grimsel Pass (7,135 f, 19½ m) —Gletsch junction for Furka, see below (5,708 f, 23 m)— Brigue (2,214 f, 52 m)—Sion (88 m)—Lausanne (148 m).

Furka

Gletsch (5,708 f)—Hotel Belvedere (7,545 f, 4½ m)—Furka Pass (7,990 f, 6 m)—Andermatt (4,737 f, 19 m).

St. Gotthard

Flüelen (1,440 f)—Wassen (3,050 f, 17 m)—Göschenen (3,640 f, 20 m)—Andermatt (4,737 f, 23 m)—St. Gotthard Pass (6,935 f, 31 m)—Airolo (3,750 f, 41 m)—Bellinzona (760 f, 77 m)—Lugano (905 f, 97 m)—Italian frontier at Chiasso (765 f, 111 m).

Susten

Wassen (3,050 f)—Susten Pass (7,420 f, 11 m)—Innertkirchen (2,106 f, 29 m)—Meiringen (1,960 f, 32 m).

Tour of the Three Passes (Susten, Grimsel, Furka), see page 180.

Oberalp Pass

Andermatt (4,737 f)—Oberalp (6,720 f, 6½ m)—Disentis (3,793 f, 19½ m)—Coire (1,925 f, 60½ m).

Klausen Pass

Altdorf (1,518 f)—Klausen Pass (6,437 f, 14½ m)—Linthal (2,136 f, 29 m)—Glarus (1,559 f, 40 m).

3. THE LAKE OF LUCERNE AND NEIGHBOURHOOD

Lucerne–Küssnacht (8 m)—Arth (13½ m)—Schwyz (21 m)—Brunnen (24 m)—Flüelen (31½ m)—Altdorf (33½ m).

Lucerne to Brunnen via Weggis (24 m).

Lucerne—Cham (13 m)—Zürich (37 m).

Lucerne—Arth (13½ m)—Einsiedeln (34 m).

Lucerne—Habsburg Castle (44 m).

Lucerne—Stansstad (11 m)—Bürgenstock (13½ m).

Lucerne—Stansstad (11 m)—Engelberg (25 m).

Lucerne—Sarnen (15 m)—Melchsee-Frutt (25 m).

INDEX

Aargau, 64
Aegeri, Lake of, 40
Ahorn, Lucas, 132
Alpnach, Stadt and Lake, 99, 100, 101, 156
Altdorf, 33, 194, 207
Amery, Leo, 71
Amiel, 128
Amsteg, 196
Amstutz, Max, 198
Andermatt, 202–208
Arnold, Matthew, 9, 199
Arnold, Thomas, 11
Arth, 166, 186
Arth-Goldau, 185
Assam, K. D. and E. Q., 216
Austria, John, Archduke of, 60
Austria, Leopold of, 37, 42
Axenstein, 178

Baar, 187
Baden, 64
Badrutt, Caspar, 159
Bagger, Eugene, 79, 82
Barrés, 22
Basel, 18, 27, 54
Beckenried, 179
Benziger, 176
Berne, 41, 48, 52, 54, 55, 60, 61, 72
Birchler, Dr. L., 190, 212
Bourbaki Panorama, 129–131
Brünig, 87–89
Brunnen, 7, 8, 169–180, 207
Bryce, Lord, 17
Buochs, 39, 40, 159
Bürgenstock, 157–161
Burke, 210
Byron, Lord, 57, 174, 185

Calame, Alexander, 160, 188
Calvin, 140
Canning, Stratford, 57–62
Castre, Edouard, 130–131
Coleridge, 56
Conolly, Cyril, 199
Coxe, Archdeacon, 103–105, 132

Dietschiberg, 162

Disentis, 208
Dufour, General, 65
Durrer, Father, 96

Einsiedeln, 39, 201, 211–222
Elliott, Doreen, 106
Engelberg, 101–106, 194
Ennetburgen, 159
Erstfeld, 194

Faenza, Charter of, 31
Felsenweg, 157
Flüelen, 6, 22, 193
Flüeli-Ranft, 90
France, relations with Switzerland, 49, 137. *See also* Napoleon, Swiss in Foreign Service
Frey-Fürst, F., 159–161
Fribourg, 52, 64
Furka Pass, 179

Garland, H. G., 170
Geneva, 48, 75, 115
Gersau, 162, 164
Gesner, Conrad, 156
Gessler, 32
Gibbon, 3, 219, 220
Giswil, 89
Glarus, 42, 44, 194
Gletsch, 208
Goethe, 3, 190, 199, 220
Göschenen, 195
Grimm, Robert, 35
Grimsel Pass, 181
Grindelwald, 114
Guedalla, P., 182
Guisan, General, 22

Habsburg, Albrecht von, 20, 37
Habsburg, Frederic von, 37
Habsburg, Leopold von, 37–41
Habsburg, Rudolf von, 18, 19, 31–32
Habsburg, Rudolf the Silent, 30–31
Habsburgs, Rise of, 17–21
Harrison, Frederic, 5, 11
Haslital, 87, 133
Heinrich VII, 30

Henry VII of Luxemburg, 37
Henry VIII of England, 134
Hergiswil, 156
Hertenstein, 163
Hodler, 131
Hogg, John, 89
Hohenstaufen Emperors, 30
Hohle Gasse, 34
Holbein, 118
Holy Roman Empire, 13–17
Honegg, 159
Hospental, 205
Hug, Mrs. Lina, 53
Huxley, Aldous, 24

Immensee, 164, 186
Interlaken, 87
Isental, 179
Isleten, 179
Ital Reding Haus, 182

James, Henry, 181, 194
Jenny, Dr., 98
Joch Pass, 106, 109

Kämpfer, Dr., 83
Kantönligeist, 75
Kappel, 46
Kehrsiten, 157
Kerns, 99
Kingsmill, Hugh, 128
Kissling, 194
Klaus, Bruder, 89–97
Klausen Pass, 194
Kleine Scheidegg, 110
Klewenalp, 179
Klösterli, 166
Knutwil, 99
Koch, Dr., 190
Küssnacht, 10, 33, 34, 163

Lamartine, 145
Laur-Belart, Dr., 204
Lausanne, 54
Lauterbrunnen, 198
Lenzburg, 17
Lepanto, Battle of, 153
Linthal, 194
Locarno, 47
Lowerz, Lake of, 185
Lucerne, Lake of, 5–11
Lucerne, Town of, 41, 55, 64,
  115–132, 147–148

Lukmanier, 28, 208
Lungern, Lake, 89

Mackintosh, Sir James, 8
Maderanertal, 75, 196–201
Malplaquet, 143
Marignano, 44, 136–137
Martin, William, 29, 46, 51, 61,
  151
Matterhorn, 165
Maximilian of Austria, 134
Mayne, Ethel Colburn, 174
Medici, Catherine de, 140
Meglinger, 126
Meiringen, 87, 106
Melchsee-Frutt, 107–114
Melchtal, Arnold von, 109
Menardy, General, 54
Mengelt, Martin, 196
Metternich, 64
Meyer, Dr. Karl, 33–35
Michelet, 199
Moos, Xaver von, 122
Moosbruger, Caspar and Joseph,
  212, 216
Moretini, Pietro, 203
More, St. Thomas, 135
Morgarten, 39–41
Müller, Herr, 208–210

Näfels, 42
Napoleon, 53–57, 145, 164, 198
Nikolaus von der Flüe, St., 89–97
Nidwalden, 102, 157
Northcote, James, 166

Obwalden, 34, 102
Ochs, Peter, 54
Oddie, Mrs., 106
Odermatt, Adolf, 106
Oeschli, Professor, 62, 65

Pace, Sir Richard, 134
Palmerston, Lord, 65
Peasants' War, 49
Pilatus, 155–157
Pfyffer, Colonel, 152
Pfyffer, Colonel Louis, 140–141
Pfyffer, General Ludwig, 119

Reding, Alois von, 55
Reding, Frau von, 182–184
Reformation in Switzerland,
  44–51

Reinhard, Herr and Frau, 111–113
Reynold, Gonzague de, 35, 51
Rigi, 165–168
Rigi Riviera, 162–168
Ruskin, John, 6, 8, 33, 38, 76, 115, 214
Rütli, 22, 179

Sachseln, 89, 95
St. Meinrad, 211
Salis, de, 142, 145
Sarnen, 98
Schiller, 169–173
Schinznach, 17
Schöllenen Gorge, 203
Schwyz, 26, 30, 34, 38, 40, 55, 64, 75, 181–186
Scott, Geoffrey, 213
Scott, Sydney, 174
Seelisberg, 179
Seewen, 185
Seiler, Alexander, 83
Sempach, 42, 117, 124
Shelley, 3, 173–176
Siegfried, André, 78
Sihl, 219
Singer, F., J., and others, 98, 99, 185
Sonderbund, The, 64
Spengler, 199
Staeger, F., 77
Stalin, 177
Stans, 101
Stanserhorn, 101
Stansstad, 40, 100, 157
Stauffacher, 33
Stephen, Leslie, 11
Stockalp, 107
Stoos, 179
Surenen Pass, 194
Susten Pass, 180
Suvoroff, 206–208
Swiss campaigns on foreign soil, 60
Swiss, civil wars of, 46, 63–66
Swiss, constitution of, 68–72
Swiss democracy, 67–77
Swiss, effect of Reformation on, 44–51

Swiss Federal Council, 71–75
Swiss flag, origin of, 133
Swiss guards at Vatican, 152–154
Swiss in foreign service, 133–154
Swiss in service of France, 136–147
Swiss life in Alpine valleys, 80–84
Swiss neutrality, 50–51, 60, 61
Swiss oligarchy, 82–84
Swiss prosperity, 77–80

Tawney, R. H., 47
Tell, William, 32–34
Tell's Chapel, 34, 163, 192
Tennyson, Alfred, 198
Thorwalden, 132
Tillendorf, 33
Titlis, 102
Trübsee, 106
Twain, Mark, 167, 192

Unterwalden, 30, 34, 64, 102
Uri, 13, 30, 33, 34, 194
Uri, Bay of, 8, 177
Uri-Rothstock, 177
Urseren, 202

Valais, 64
Vallière, Major P. de, 139–154
Vaud, 54–55
Victoria, Queen, 205
Views, best in Alps, 165
Vitznau, 164

Wagner, 126–129, 177
Wassen, 195
Watteville, De, 142
Weggis, 162–163
Weissenstein, 165
Wickham, William, 54, 206
Wilde, Oscar, 4
Williman, Herr, 176
Winkelried, Arnold von, 101
Wolfenschiessen, 101
Wordsworth, Dorothy, 87, 103, 166, 184
Wordsworth, William, 56, 87, 101, 103
Wyl, Jacob, 126

Zug, town and lake, 187–191
Zürich, 44–47
Zürich, Lake of, 151
Zwingli, 44–46, 151